How to Grade Your Professors

And Other Unexpected Advice

How to Grade Your Professors

And Other Unexpected Advice

Jacob Neusner

Beacon Press Boston

Beacon Press books are published under the auspices
of the Unitarian Universalist Association of
Congregations in North America,
25 Beacon Street, Boston, Massachusetts 02108
Published simultaneously in Canada by
Fitzhenry and Whiteside Limited, Toronto

Printed in the United States of America

(hardcover) 9 8 7 6 5 4 3 2 1
(paperback) 9 8 7 6 5 4 3 2

Library of Congress Cataloging in Publication Data

Neusner, Jacob, 1932–
  Includes Index.
  1. Universities and colleges—United States.
2. College students—United States. 3. Education, Higher
—United States. I. Title. II. Title. III. Title:
LA227.3.N38 1984   378.73   84–45081
ISBN 0–8070–3152–6
ISBN 0–8070–3153–4 (pbk.)

For
my undergraduate students
at
Columbia University, 1960–1961
University of Wisconsin-Milwaukee, 1961–1962
Dartmouth College, 1964–1968
Brown University, 1968–1984

"Much have I learned from my teachers,
"Still more from my colleagues,
"But most of all from my students."

And among them all,
especially for
Ted Kovaleff, Columbia '64
William S. Green, Dartmouth '68
Thomas J. Tisch, Brown '76

More than teachers, these became my dearest friends.

Contents

Preface

HIS IS A PROFOUNDLY CONSERVATIVE book and a deeply radical one. Addressing students and their parents, I mean to defend and to conserve the freedom from cant and snobbery and the freedom to learn attained in the campus revolution of the 1960s and 1970s. I believe the classical values of the world's great traditions of learning — transcending the universities and the West — found expression in the changes of that time. At the same time I propose to take a fresh look at what goes on behind the ivied walls of American colleges and universities and offer a set of observations that, to some, will seem a radical critique, coming as they do from a university professor. The critique pertains to how we teach and what we call research. I mean to offer a vision and a dream. These, by definition, are always radical. Some critics condemn the freedom to choose courses and shape one's own curriculum, a freedom attained on many campuses a decade and a half ago and today severely curtailed. I want to celebrate that freedom. But it is freedom to learn rigorously, to do more than we thought we could, to transform learning into discovery, education into a quest for responsibility and maturity in mind and heart. The outcome of the 1960s and 1970s yielded greater rigor, more demands for discipline in learning and for hard work in education. Today we are free to surpass ourselves, to do better than we thought we could.

The legacy of the 1960s and 1970s for the students of the 1980s and 1990s remains to be sorted out. Some claim that the advent of new groups on the campus — blacks typify them — diminished the excellence of the universities. I maintain the opposite. Universities serve society more effectively now than when they were bastions of privilege and prejudice. Learning overcomes bigotry, so colleges should not reinforce it. They are better than they were. Some allege that the emphasis on drawing into the scholarly professions formerly excluded groups — women represent these groups — lowered standards of achievement among faculties. I argue the opposite. Universities draw upon deeper resources of talent and broader ranges of imagination and opinion now than they did when white males of a certain caste of society (and outcasts who imitated them) defined what was, and what was not, worth thinking: what was classical. These two achievements of the revolution in higher education stand for much else. They represent permanent steps forward, irrevocable policies to open and strengthen colleges and universities.

But these changes confronted students and the campus with a long period of adjustment and accommodation. Colleges and universities are emerging from a period of change. The certainties of an earlier age, set aside in the unsettling events of the later 1960s and 1970s, must now be examined. Debate on the conduct of higher education returns to once-rejected issues, such as matters of requirements and authority, standards and values. In earlier days, before the era of a cultural revolution on the campus, everyone knew what we were doing. During the time of change, everyone concurred that we did not. Now the certainties, both the old and the more recent, fade — an exciting time.

College students and their parents confront professors less certain of their tasks than any in memory. Yet students and their parents in a brief interval of four years must take up the tasks, set for them by the same professors, meant to attain the goals that higher education has always set for itself. How is anyone to know what to do, and where to do it, when those who are supposed to know agree on little? Students and parents cannot wait while professors pick their way through the chaos that confronts them. Young people come and study and leave, now as before; they cannot choose to learn from a particular generation of professors.

My qualifications to offer guidance to students and counsel to parents are two. I am a parent, and I am a professor. I wrote this book because I discovered, as the parent of college-bound sons and a daughter, that I suffered as much as everyone else from the anguish of the age. I needed guidance in order to know what my children should do. I went to college thirty years ago — and never left. Yet how could I tell good from mediocre, worthwhile from pretentious and empty on the campus? I knew little better than my neighbors, who are not professors, even though I know a great many more facts about universities than they do.

Indeed, I joined one of the educationally most radical colleges in the country at its moment of crisis and renewal. I arrived at Brown University in 1968, just when the university adopted a curriculum based on the theory that no requirements except those for a major promised freedom to choose intelligently and that punitive measures in the classroom — an emphasis on exams and grades, for instance — produced less enlightenment than would an attitude of shared responsibility. I believe the theory behind this new curriculum is sound, if occasionally flawed in practice, and I think this university is a better place than it has ever been. Yet, when my own children were ready to go to college, I wanted something else for my particular son, with his distinctive educational needs. How was I to find what he needed and how was I to know it when he and I had found it? In the tradition of my own university, I left the matter mainly up to him, and he made a very good choice indeed.

In this book I want to share with high school seniors, college freshmen, and their perplexed parents what I have learned in nearly a quarter of a century of college teaching. I want to speak to my sons and daughter and their generation of high school and college students. It already is clear that I do not have the wisdom to solve the problems at hand: Where should I send my child to college? Should I do it at all? Why not? Why so? What is a university and what work does it do and why should my child spend four years in such a place?

Here I assume that students and parents know as little as I did when I changed from professor to parent. I give answers to those questions people assume we have already answered, explaining as briefly and as objectively as I can just what a professor is and does, as well as others whom the public will meet on a college or university campus. I take as the analogy for my task the work of explaining to a prospective world traveler just what will happen, whom the traveler will see, what the traveler will observe. Everybody assumes we know all about other parts of the world — until we get there. Then we are surprised and confused. So too with higher education. We all know what we want and how to get it, until we arrive there with our cherished daughters and sons. Then the stakes go up, and we realize that any information we can glean will strengthen our hand.

In this book I look as critically as I can, with all the passion I can muster, at the single institution to which I have devoted my life, and at the one thing in American society I believe makes a difference for the long-term future. I criticize because I care. I ask the coming generation of students and their parents to care too. Your futures are at issue — and in doubt.

I started writing this book on a journey to a far-off place, in quest of a distant time. I had gone in search of a perspective on the world that I, through teaching, help to frame — I mean, America and the West. I wrote the first chapters on the shores of the Karawari River, a tributary of the Sepik, the great river of Papua New Guinea. Looking out from a hillside across fifty miles of jungle, at night without electricity, in daytime without the familiar Rhode Island trees, birds, people, I reflected on the everyday. So far from the green in the distance, the blue skies above, the mud and the insects and the exotic flowers round about, my mind reflected on how different things can be from how they are. What moved me was not the unity of the other with us, but the choices that all of us have the power to make. For even in the jungle people do make choices and change the world in which they live. All the more so can we choose in a world accustomed to choice and change.

Individuals do have the power to shape their lives, to make and carry out important decisions on the kind of people they will be. They do not have to repeat their mistakes. Seeing how one group differed from another in that most diverse of all countries, with its seven hundred languages and peoples — a quarter of the known languages on the face of the earth — I realized how much we as individuals can do.

This is a book about how things should be, how they are, and where and why we can change them. I tell the story of the critical phase of beginning lives and careers, the phase of college education. But I mean to make (never merely to score) points. This book has a thesis and intends to lay down significant judgments. If I can persuade readers that colleges and universities compare, not to the jungle and the sky and the mountains, just there, forever, unchanging to our eye, but to what we ourselves manufacture or accept, the mud and the flies and smoky huts down below, I shall have made a point worth setting forth: We are responsible for what we do.

I mean to guide high school and college students as they approach and proceed through the next, and for most the final, phase of formal education, the passage to and through colleges and universities. What are these places? Who works in them? What purpose do they serve? What happens in them from season to season and from year to year? I hope to raise the sights of students and their parents, to outline what I conceive to be a program and a plan of education, where and how it happens. I aim at a vision worthy of those students and their parents, deserving of the wealth in humanity and in hope, in the precious years of youth and in the precious dollars of middle age spent on us — the professors — and on the things we do in universities. If we who make up colleges and universities prove worthy of those human and material gifts, in the end our work will prove to be our country's salvation.

Two other sorts of books belong alongside this one, because I do not cover certain topics. First, students should consult the many good guides to facts about individual colleges and universities. Second, parents and teachers will find extensive discussion of higher education, such as methods for raising standards of learning and other problems, in newspapers, magazines, and books. My book will not cover these specific topics. I want to offer guidance and reflection — a vision of how things should be, an account of how an experienced professor sees college now.

If this book succeeds in its task, high school students will approach college more knowledgeably, and college students will work their way through their first two or three years more reflectively, with a sharper perspective on what they are doing. If you find this book helpful, write me a letter and tell me. More important, if you give me the advantage of your criticism and counsel, you will help me improve this book in future editions. I cannot solve everybody's problems, but I can try to learn from everybody and share the lessons.

Jacob Neusner

Brown University
Providence, Rhode Island

March 15, 1984
Our twentieth wedding anniversary.
It seems like forever. Was there a
before? Can there be an afterward?

Acknowledgments

HIS BOOK WAS THE IDEA OF ALLEN FIT-
chen, director of the University of Wiscon-
sin press, when he was my editor at the
University of Chicago Press. Both of us were
sending first sons to college, and I remarked
to him that, as a professor, I was not a very
good parent. I could not advise my son about any aspect of
choosing a college (nor did he want to take my advice). Mr.
Fitchen said, "Well, why don't you write a book about it? I
mean, 'parent and professor.'" So I tried.

The book that resulted is not the one you are reading now.
It took a great editor to see that what I had written might be
made relevant to a larger world and even to the moment at
hand. Wendy Strothman, director of Beacon Press, deserves
whatever credit accrues to this book. She is the best editor
I have ever known, and I have worked with many good ones.
She saw the right way to organize my ideas and she guided
me to a mode of approaching the problems at hand that
rendered public and intelligible what began as an essentially
private experience. Since the manuscript was rejected by no
fewer than ten university presses (including Mr. Fitchen's),
as well as more than a score of education, trade, and com-
mercial publishers, I owe everything to Ms. Strothman and
Beacon.

If I was encouraged to persist in thinking I had something
of worth to say to others, it was because of the encouragement of my wife, Suzanne Richter Neusner, who read the
earliest manuscript, and my friends, Thomas Tisch and William

Green, as well as William Green's wife, Rebecca Fox, who read successive ones.

And yet, as the dedication indicates, what I have learned about college and college teaching comes to me from my best teachers, my students. From their papers and examinations every year I see how I have failed. But in their lives I sometimes see a spark of a teacher's success. I have had a difficult career. But because of the pleasure of students, from year to year, I never regretted choosing to live as only a teacher and only a scholar, and I never imagined any other way of life. More than that I cannot offer in praise and thanks to the students of the past twenty-five years.

In college students do two important things. First, they learn. Second, they grow up. I have had the privilege of learning and growing with students for a quarter of a century. The dedication presents a token of my thanks.

Introduction

NIVERSITIES AND COLLEGES PRESENT a special predicament to the public at large. The public pays the university enormous respect but also treats it to profound neglect. When, after all, do people see universities? It is commonly at graduation time, when everybody feels wonderful, and no one wants to ask hard questions. In the color and drama of commencement ceremonies, the public celebrates these marvelous places, these incomparable centers of learning and tradition, these pillars of society and founders and framers of the future generations. The memory of graduation day pomp and excitement colors the whole year.

It is as if people always viewed the presidency through a vision of the White House at night, or the president as he is on inauguration day. With the power of ceremonial good will, presidents would rule forever. For much of the general public, that is how universities appear as they reign in the cultural and educational affairs of the country. They dispose, they decide, they determine which thoughts are thinkable and which are not, what history is and is not, what science will investigate and what it will not. In learning there is no other significant countervailing force, no balance of powers with a Congress and a judiciary against which, and with which, the university must struggle for validation and effect.

Universities define the history of the civilization of the West, beginning at the point in European history at which the world as we know it began to take shape. Theirs is the dream of what society can be, theirs is the vision of what humanity is. It is a profoundly radical dream of a world in which intelligence matters, a deeply conservative vision of the irreducible worth of the human person, a libertarian appreciation of what each individual thinks and feels and becomes. But colleges and universities are what we make them. They are supposed to shelter learning and nurture minds. They also may provide a cover for politics, protection for mediocrity, a seedbed for self-indulgence. Professors read books and write papers, or give assignments and correct examinations. But these activities often bear little relationship to education. A modest compact of deceit and self-deceit joins too many professors and students in defense of mediocrity: Only a few people work hard, but everyone is rewarded. And who loses? Who indeed, but the wasted teacher, the cheated student, above all the society — America — that needs the best from all of us.

And yet that is not my message. This is a book of perfect faith in the promise of these disappointing colleges and universities. They do not always have to be what they now are. It is not only that the stakes are high. It is also that the people who come to them, our sons and daughters, and the people who constitute them, we professors, together form a community of considerable promise. To what other age than youth is given the leisure to learn? To what other profession than college teacher is given the privilege of educating others in their mature years — introducing and exploring ideas and their implications, and being paid for it? Ours is a remarkable opportunity, an amazing occasion, an honor, a privilege few others enjoy. Only parents compare to us as creators and founders of the future. But we are paid, and we see our students only when we may prove useful to them. No one pays parents, and they cannot set their own hours. So if I point out duplicity and laziness and missed opportunities, it is because of the promise and the hope at hand. As a religious person, I indulge myself in a single prayer: May I be worthy of my privileges.

Part One

The Ideal and the Dream

Chapter One
The Dream and the Vision

I N FRESHMAN WEEK IN SEPTEMBER 1972, at the height of the cultural revolution in American higher education, I spoke to the entering students in my university. The promise and the power of that hour, when everything seems new to freshmen and all things seem possible in an American college, set the task at hand. I had to explain to a new generation what aspects of the worthy past had lasted and would last. The explanation required, not defense, but advocacy of ideals. For the past always dies, unless the generation that follows takes up what it considers worthwhile and adopts as its own what others have learned. The message of that unsettling time frames what I conceive to be the goal of learning even in more placid times.

The students were many and, I felt, ready to listen for at least twenty minutes. The room was bright, the sun was in my eyes; I could scarcely make out faces in the glare. It was just as well. I meant to speak impersonally, with a message of an ancient, ever-renewed world.

This is what I say to prospective college students and to freshmen as they begin their higher education. Let me say it in the same words I used on that day in 1972.

"This week marks the commencement of your four years at this university. My purpose is to introduce those four years.

"You come to take your places in an ongoing enterprise, a university. It was here before you came. It probably will be here after you leave. But you can and will make your mark upon it. You can enhance its life, or blight its future. Each generation of faculty, students, and administrators has that power. For universities are fragile. They rise and fall, go through periods of excellence and mediocrity. This you already know, for you applied to many universities and colleges and chose the best for you, so you realize that significant differences separate one university from another. We have no truth-in-advertising law to cover universities; they all call themselves by the same name. But the differences are there, and in the next four years, you are one of the givens, one of the data, that will characterize and distinguish this university from others.

"But your first impression must be different. As you enter this university, you must perceive yourselves to be the last and least in a long procession of men and women. You see buildings you did not build, a great library, carefully nurtured for two hundred years, that you did not create, a faculty you did not assemble, a community you did not form. Everything seems so well established, so permanent. But that impression is illusory.

"Just a few years ago students in universities burned and ravaged the buildings designed for their use, closed the libraries, shut down the classrooms. Clearly students have the power to destroy.

"By their excellence students also have the power to build. Faculties come to teach the best students they can find; high salaries and pleasant working conditions alone do not suffice to keep talented men and women in universities composed of bored and sullen students. If you are purposeful, if you are mindful, if you are critical, thoughtful, interested students, you will give the university the good name of a place where the life of thought and ideas is fully and richly lived. And within my experience, our university's greatest asset is its students. I cannot exaggerate the excellence, the charm, of the students I have known here, and I do not speak for myself alone.

"So do not see yourselves as unimportant. Your coming is important; it is the decisive event of the present. What other generations have created, the wealth they have lavished on this place, the care and concern they have given it, the endowment of centuries, are opportunities now fallen into your hands. Do not waste what other men and women have made. Do not take for granted the unearned increment of the ages. For four years you live on the labor of other, earlier generations, who gave to the future what they in turn had received from the past.

"What happens in this university? First, let me say what does not happen. The problems of the world are not going to be solved by you. You are not coming here to make a better world, to improve the condition of humankind, or to solve the problem of poverty. Indeed, the money that society (not to mention your parents) spends on you here is diverted from other worthwhile projects. The endowment of this university could purchase better housing for many of the poor or raise the welfare benefits for many of the needy. But it is set aside so that you, mature men and women perfectly capable of working at some useful and remunerative task, may remain idle. You are kept unemployed, and others have to pay for your keep, so that you may read books, work in labs, listen and talk, write and think.

"A university is an expression of a highly aristocratic, anti-egalitarian ideal; it stands for the opposite of the equality of all men and women, for their inequalities in matters of the mind and spirit. A great many people past and present have set aside their wealth and their energies for the aristocratic ideal that excellent minds have the opportunity for growth and improvement, that the intellect be cultivated. Your years here could just as easily be spent on more socially relevant purposes. You could, after all, take a job and earn a living for yourselves. But you sacrifice that income. Your four years of apparent idleness represent a joint decision, by you and your family and 'society,' that at the moment it is better to think so that later you may do; it is wiser now to hold back so that later you may go much farther onward.

"Yet the activity that will not take place at this university — your immediate engagement with the great tasks of society — imposes on you an extraordinary struggle: the struggle to postpone easy accomplishment and quick distinction. True achievement depends on depth of learning, on capacity for clear thinking, on ability to pursue knowledge where curiosity leads, above all on implacable criticism of all givens. True achievement depends on these things, rather than on the premature acceptance of public responsibility. Young men and women want to go forth, to do great things. We keep you here to study, to think about things. You come full of energy. You would find it natural to take on great tasks. You want nothing less than to sit long hours in the discipline of the mind. To read and write, to argue and expound, to confront the various claims to truth in a sophisticated, critical spirit — these represent stern tests for men and women at your age (or any other). You are called to an unnatural repression of your personal selves, to overcome the natural instincts of your age.

"Nothing is so hard as seeing your contemporaries at their life's work and postponing your own. You represent only a small proportion of your age group. The majority will not be with you this fall; many are at work, or at considerably less demanding universities than this one. Nothing is so inviting as picking up the burdens of the world and entering the workaday life, nor so demanding of self-discipline as denying them. You come to learn, not with the curious but empty minds of preteens, but the strength of maturing, able men and women. The conquest of the self — by overcoming ambition, distraction, and sheer laziness, and by bringing your best abilities to the service of the mind — will prove most satisfying of all conquests for those of you who achieve it. Later on no enemy will prove so difficult as the enemy within. No challenge will prove harder to meet than the one you now meet within yourself. In the university you have now to vanquish the undisciplined impulse to ready yourself for struggle with, for service to, the world.

"Above all, if you succeed in acquiring the critical mode of thought that is our ware, you will have the one thing you will need to become important people: the capacity to stand firm in what you think right, in what you propose to accomplish in life. Today you have to postpone the quest for worldly success. Later on that success may not come; you may have to walk quite by yourself. When the world is against you, you will have to rely for strength only upon your own convictions. I speak from experience: The world is not going to give you many satisfactions, especially if you propose to change it. For if you do, you thereby claim things are not yet perfect. What everybody thinks is true really is not so. What everybody wants to do, thinks it right and best to do, is not the best way at all. Great men and women achieve their greatness above the mob, not within it. And they cannot be loved on that account.

"The world will love its own, those who tell and do the things reassuring to the mediocre. Here you begin to struggle with the given, with the natural, with how you feel and how your friends feel. Do not expect the success that comes from easy accomplishment and ready recognition. What will justify the effort if all there is before you is defeat and renewed struggle? You must not learn to expect success in order to justify your efforts. You must learn to need only to think the effort necessary, whatever the outcome. Great things are not accomplished by the shouters but by the workers. But to learn to work — that is a hard task indeed.

"I have said what will not happen here. What then does happen here? Only one achievement makes worthwhile the years and money you devote to your university education: You should learn to ask questions and to find the answers to them. Everything else is frivolous, peripheral, for the shouters and the headline chasers. And a great many of the questions you will ask and learn to answer are irrelevant to shouting and to headlines.

"Now, what are these questions? They are not the generalities but the specificities, not the abstractions but the concrete and detailed matters that delimit the frontiers of knowledge. Do not ask, what is a human being? or What is truth? or What is history? or What is biology? Your teachers may give you answers to these great questions, but the answers are routine. And your teachers cannot tell you the value of the answer. What we want is only to *know*: not necessarily how to harness atomic energy, but about energy and matter, not necessarily how to 'cure cancer,' but about the nature of living matter.

"Notice I did not say we seek the truth but only the truth *about* . . . I mean to emphasize the tentativeness, the modesty, the austerity of our work. I begin, after all, as a critic of my own perceptions; only then do I criticize those of others. In what I do I seek to know the limits of knowledge, to define just what is factual about the facts purportedly in my hands. For the asking of questions, the seeking of answers, begins in a deep skepticism. If I thought we knew all we need to know, what should I find to ask? The asking of questions is a subversive activity. It subverts accepted truths, the status quo.

"Your teachers here do not propose to tell you what is generally agreed upon as the truth about this or that subject. In this regard you must not assume they are like your teachers in high school or prep school, teachers who were responsible for communicating established knowledge, for teaching you what is already agreed upon. Your teachers in college are different because they are actively engaged in the disciplined study and questioning of the given. They are trying to find out new things, trying to reassess the truth of the old. The high school teacher you already know tends to take for granted the correctness of what he or she tells you. The teachers here are going to ask whether what they tell you is so, how they claim to know it, and, above all, *how they have found it out.* They are active participants in learning, not passive recipients and transmitters of other people's facts. How they think, how they analyze a problem, therefore, is what you have to learn from them. It is all they have to teach you. What they think you probably can find out in books, mine or someone else's. Why they think so — this alone they can tell you. Before now, in high school, the result of learning was central. Here, in college, the modes and procedures of thinking are at issue.

"I said earlier that what makes your years here important is the asking of questions and the finding of answers. But there is a second important process, flowing from the first, in which you must learn to participate: the process of communication. It is not enough to have found ways of thought. One has to express them as well. As the great Yale historian Edmund S. Morgan says, 'Scholarship begins in curiosity, but it ends in communication.' You do not need to justify asking questions. But if you think you have found answers, you do not have the right to remain silent. I do not guarantee people will listen to you. The greater likelihood is that they will ignore what they do not understand or vilify what they do not like. Nevertheless, you are not free from the task of saying what you think. This will take two forms, and you must master both: writing and speaking. You must learn to express your ideas in a clear and vigorous way. You must do this both in writing and in discussions in the classroom (and outside as well). I promise you that your teachers will give you many opportunities to exercise and improve your skills at both.

"On the importance of communicating ideas as the center of the educational experience, let me again quote Edmund Morgan:

> Communication is not merely the desire and responsibility of the scholar; it is his discipline. . . . Without communication his pursuit of truth withers into eccentricity. He necessarily spends much of his time alone. . . . But he needs to be rubbing constantly against other minds. . . . He needs to be made to explain himself. . . . The scholar . . . needs company to keep him making sense . . . people to challenge him at every step, who will take nothing for granted.

Morgan said these words to a freshman class at Yale, and he ended, 'In short, he needs you.'

"And this brings me back to where I started, your importance to this university. You are our reason for being, not because you will listen passively and write down uncritically, but because without you there is no reason to speak or to write. What happens in the classroom is not the impersonal delivery of facts, but the analysis of possibilities and probabilities by concerned people, teacher and student alike. Learning is not a passive process. A timid person cannot learn. An impatient person cannot teach. Learning is a shared experience. Without students, who is a teacher? More than the calf wants to suck the mother's milk, the cow wants to suckle that calf. I do not mean to suggest you have nothing to do but sit back, hear what a teacher has to say, and announce why he or she is wrong, or why you do not agree. That childish conception bears slight resemblance to what is to be done. I mean you have to learn things for your part, and ask questions of your own perceptions, as much as of your teacher's: It is a shared quest, a collective skepticism.

"What is the measure of success? How will you know, in four years, whether or not you have wisely spent your time here? First, you should have a good grasp of one specific field of learning, not solely the data of such a field, though they are important, but the way that field works, how specialists think within it, and why.

"Second, you should have mastered three skills that mark the educated man and woman: how to listen attentively, how to think clearly, and how to write accurately. To be sure, the modes of thought and the means of writing or other forms of expression will differ from one field to the next. But in general all modes of thought and expression will exhibit a concern for accuracy, clarity, precision, order, lucid argumentation.

"Third, you should feel slightly discontented, discontented with yourselves and therefore capable of continued growth; discontented with your field at work and therefore capable of critical judgement and improvement; discontented with the world at large and therefore capable of taking up the world's task as a personal and individual challege.

"You come not merely to spend four years in a world you have not made and for which you therefore do not bear responsibility. You come to join and build a community, a community of scholars. If the experience of community is meaningful to you, you will, wherever you may be, never really leave it. You will continue to participate in the scholarly enterprise — asking questions, finding answers, telling people about them."

If I had to summarize my introduction to college in one sentence, I would describe the goal of a college education in this way: (1) don't ask, discover, therefore (2) take responsibility for your life and your mind, so that (3) you will live a well-examined life. I do not know any other institution in society that sets for itself the goal of turning out better human beings. True, no other institution fails as often or as miserably as we do. But think of the successes! College is a place of friendship, of making friends through life, among people with whom you share a task and a purpose, but it is also a place to encounter a new and adult world. This is one way of beginning.

Chapter Two

Learning and Growing Up

'JUST CAN'T TAKE HOLD, MOM. I CAN'T take hold of some kind of a life.'' That is what Biff says to his mother in Arthur Miller's play *Death of a Salesman*, and that, I believe, expresses a fundamental concern of our students. Students come to college not only to learn but also to grow up. They leave their homes, or if they continue to live there, they assert their independence in other ways. At the same time they do not take up the tasks of the workaday world. They rarely support themselves but depend in some measure upon others, whether parents or universities. Students come to us, in the main, at the last stage of childhood, toward the end of adolescence, and they leave us, in the main, as mature men and women. During the four swift years between, they have to solve the last problem of their earlier life and the first of the life beyond: Who am I? During this time, they declare a moratorium on making firm decisions and begin a period of subdued inner searching. They play many roles in this period, experimenting with each of them in search of a place in society, a niche, as Erik Erikson says in *Identity: Youth and Crisis*, ''which is firmly defined and yet seems to be uniquely made'' for them.

The time of college education marks a way station between the complete dependence of a child and the total independence of an adult. What do people do during this interim period? They study various subjects. How does what they study relate to the process of maturing? This is a crucial question for professors. If we cannot relate the encounter with learning in college to the student's experiment in defining an identity, we ignore that is truly essential. If I can show that what we do — that is, learning a subject in a particular way — is critical to what the students want to become, mature and independent women and men, then I will realize the ideal of the college experience.

Students arrive in college thinking they know the answers to certain basic questions — What am I doing here? Why now? Why me? Then they find out they do not know the answers. They have the difficult task of shaping an adult identity. But where should they do this? Why in college in particular? Simple logic demands that if you are in college, you study subjects of higher education. But if these subjects do not relate to that other important task — growing up — then there will be tension between what the student is learning and what the student has to accomplish in personal growth.

Since much is asked of each student, and much is expected by those who send young people to college, a student's inability to find answers to those questions of purpose will lead to a sense of betrayal and shame. The students will feel they have betrayed those who helped them go to college — parents and high school teachers. They will feel ashamed of themselves. Rather than endure either of these feelings, they may retreat within, to the protected world of their peer group, avoiding a confrontation with the disturbing and distressing issues of a larger world. They will move insensately from classroom to dormitory, from dining hall to the movies (rarely to the library), in the company of others like themselves.

I do not exaggerate the consequences of the inability to find a bridge between learning and maturing. If anything, I understate them. Many students find exceedingly difficult the discovery of what relates their personal problems and concerns — the problems of growth and the discovery of identity — to the questions they ask themselves as university students.

It is easy to pretend the issue is an illusion. Many students are able to give a clear-cut answer to the questions, Why are you at college? What do you seek in this classroom? Those students who have (for the moment) declared themselves premedical, prelegal, or preprofessional solve the problem without ever facing it during the college years. But the solution will not serve. The problem is only postponed to a less propitious time. And identity is not the same thing as knowing how one plans to make a living five, ten, or twenty years from now. A preprofessional commitment in the liberal arts setting is an evasion, not an answer, to the questions, Why here? Why now? Why me? These questions add up to a single one: Who am I?

Questions are addressed to their teachers as well. Why are you telling us these things? What is important for us? What is relevant to us in your lessons? If few students know the answers, still fewer professors are able to help. For between professors and students there is a conflict not only of interest but also of orientation. A teacher's work is to criticize, to rethink established knowledge. The goal is to come to a finer and more critical perception of learning and, inevitably, to a carefully circumscribed segment of knowledge. In part, the faculty member has to communicate what he or she is learning; that communication is central to the teacher's work within the university. But a university is what it is because men and women work through what others accept as truth; they make their own, through the power of the intellect, what others may take at face value. Unfortunately, this sometimes gives us the appearance of learning more and more about less and less.

The conflict between professor and student actually revolves around very specific issues. Secure in an identity formed through the years, the professor strives to solve an external problem, alert to his or her and to others' ignorance.

Further, the work is conducted as part of a life that includes a distinguished personal history, including relationships of love and of responsibility to a larger world. To this, students offer only a contrast. Their problems are subjective and are resolved as their identity becomes clear. As they struggle with their problems they are barely aware of their ignorance. Students enjoy little past and almost no personal history; most are not married and do not make a living for themselves.

What brings men and women whose problems are those of maturity together with adolescents who are not yet certain about what problems they are going to confront? Why do professors with answers seek students who are unsure of the questions?

For the student, confronting and taking seriously a person well along the path of life can stimulate a greater maturity. Certainly, meeting men and women who sincerely hold that what is important in life need bear no relationship to material comfort, who earn less than they might in other callings, who work much harder than they would in other professions and yet do not think they "work" at all — to meet such people is apt to have salutary benefits, to offer a vivid example of how life may be lived. For the teacher, the student's fundamental question about the worth and use of knowledge is necessary, for such questions lead back to the basics of a subject; and it is there that true insight is found. The student, if open to the answers to his or her questions, will vivify the life of the teacher.

The primary goal of the student is to reach out toward an adult identity. What does the student actually do? A student's everyday life consists of attending lectures and participating in discussions, reading books, writing papers, working in laboratories — of devoting most of the day to the disciplines of the mind. One may do these things in form, and many students do. One can go through the motions of learning; indeed one may well learn a great many things. Yet if learning is irrelevant to one's personal situation, then the forms are formalities; the center; the spirit; will be lacking. And nothing that is learned will matter.

What is the relationship between learning and maturing, between study and the formation of a strong and autonomous personality? Through learning — mastery of that part of human experience accessible in books and laboratories — we both prepare for life and engage in living. Learning is liberating, not merely by relieving us of ignorance, but by supplying us with understanding and insight, with knowledge of the reality in which, and against which, we form our sense of self. There can be no purpose in the discovery of the self without the exploration of the context in which the self takes shape. Liberal learning brings the person out of the self and leads to an encounter with other people, their yearnings and complexities.

Through the record of civilization — that is, through the part of human life preserved in books and enshrined in permanent sources of knowledge — we confront the collective and accumulated experience of vast numbers of people. Repeatedly in these materials, in the legal documents or in the tales for pleasure, we find a record of earlier men and women grappling with the same problems. L. Joseph Stone and Joseph Church, in *Childhood and Adolescence: A Psychology of the Growing Person*, write, "It is, after all, in literature, with its power of enlisting strong identifications, that we learn the profoundest lessons about human relationships and the nature of social institutions. The scientist and the philosopher have been grappling for years with exactly the cosmic problems that intrigue and frighten the adolescent." In college the student finds new avenues to explore in the search for answers and new minds struggling with the same issues.

Behind all that we do as students and scholars are the three great components of reality: humanity, society, and nature. These are the center of our curriculum in the humanities, social sciences, and natural sciences. For all our impersonal devotion to our several subjects, good teachers do not forget the central issue of study: the understanding of humankind, of the complex structures formed by men and women, and of the natural setting of our brief life together on earth.

I cannot think of a more promising opportunity than that presented by this curious conflict between the subjectivity of the student and the objectivity of the teacher, between the excessive self-obsession of the young and the equally excessive submergence of self by the mature person. Neither is wholly true; each must correct the other. The teacher must draw the student out of his or her personal preoccupation in part by demonstrating the shared nature of that experience among many men and women, alive and dead; but in greater part by introducing concerns and questions, interests and commitments, currently lacking yet important and relevant to self-identification.

Let us look specifically at what this relationship between teacher and student can mean. Let us consider as an example the subject I teach, which is the history of Judaism, an old and honored religious tradition. I teach both Christian and Jewish students. The Christian students want to know about that old religion, some because of their correct belief that Christianity emerged from Judaism, many simply because it is an interesting religion. The Jewish students have a different motive. They are part of a minority, and they wonder why they should not join the majority. Their religious tradition makes demands on them, makes them different, limits their choice, for instance, of a marriage partner and restricts their diet. The Jewish students want to know why they should be Jewish. When they come to me, they perceive that I teach not *about Judaism* but Judaism, and conflict arises. They want to be told why they should be Jewish. I want to tell them what makes Judaism a complex and interesting religion, within the context of a larger study of religion. They have a deeply personal problem to work out, and I have a profoundly objective inquiry to carry on. This is a conflict of interests, a conflict between my interests and those of my students. The students introduce issues of self-identification. They rightly insist that I teach, not impersonally, but personally to Peter and Jennifer and Steve, who are deeply concerned. And they remind me that this "interesting thing" is a religion that real people live by and die for. And yet, if students only want to know what is relevant to themselves, it is hard to see what role learning and teaching can play in their growth. We are intellectuals. We insist upon analysis and interpretation, not solely upon feeling and commitment.

In this conflict of interests is the resolution. The student must draw the teacher back from the pretense of objectivity and the claim to indifference to the human meaning of his or her learning. The student serves the teacher well by asking, What does this mean to me? or What ought this to mean? And in attempting to answer, despite the frailty and impermanence of the answer, the teacher will serve the student too.

At the very center of things is this: The scholar and the adolescent have in common the capacity to look with fresh eyes on a stale world. The student is full of idealism, can see the future ahead, is not tired or jaded, and has high hopes for himself or herself and for the world. Professors also take a fresh look at old perceptions, an idealism that says that things not of this world are important. We take on the task of rethinking what everyone takes for granted, just as the student does.

We ask ourselves the most fundamental questions about the part of the world or of human experience that forms our study, just as the student asks basic questions about world, experience, and self. We too have high hopes, both for learning and for the people who learn what we think through. For the scholar is loyal to a vision, and youth is the time of vision and dreaming. And the scholar is, in the nature of things, granted the blessing of a continuing encounter with youth. No profession enjoys a greater privilege than ours, for our work is with and for students, who are our future.

The themes of our curriculum must pertain to the issues of the student's unfolding consciousness. But even more; the very method and substance of our work, the persistent, tenacious asking of basic questions, correspond in a close and direct way to the very substance and method of the student's task. The scholar's mode of thought is congruent with the adolescent's personal search. The search for relevance to one's own concerns, pursued self-consciously with a measure of restraint, must lead to the scholar's mode of study.

Chapter Three

Grading Your Professors

INCE PROFESSORS STAND AT THE CEN-
ter of the student's encounter with college
learning, students ought to ask what marks
a good professor, what indicates a bad one.
The one who sets high standards and persists
in demanding that students try to meet them
provides the right experiences. The professor who gives praise
cheaply or who pretends to a relationship that does not and
cannot exist teaches the wrong lessons. True, the demanding
and the critical teacher does not trade in the currency students
possess, which is their power to praise or reject teachers. The
demanding professor knows that students will stumble. But
the ones who pick themselves up and try again — whether
in politics or music or art or sports — have learned a lesson
that will save them for a lifetime: A single failure is not the
measure of any person, and success comes hard. A banal truth,
but a truth all the same.

The only teacher who taught me something beyond information, who gave me something to guide my life, was the
only teacher who read my work carefully and criticized it in
detail. To that point everyone had given me A's. After that
I learned to criticize myself and not to believe the A's. The
teacher who read my writing and corrected not so much the
phrasing as the mode of thought — line by line, paragraph by
paragraph, beginning to end — and who composed paragraphs
as models for what I should be saying is the sole true teacher
I ever had. But I did not need more than one, and neither do
you.

I do not mean to suggest that for each one of us there is one perfect teacher who changes our lives and is the only teacher we need. We must learn from many teachers as we grow up and grow old; and we must learn to recognize the good ones. The impressive teacher of one's youth may want to continue to dominate — as teachers do — and may not want to let go. The great teacher is the one who wants to become obsolete in the life of the student. The good teacher is the one who teaches lessons and moves on, celebrating the student's growth. The Talmud relates the story of a disciple in an academy who won an argument over the position held by God in the academy on high. The question is asked, "What happened in heaven that day?" The answer: "God clapped hands in joy, saying, 'My children have vanquished me, my children have vanquished me.' " That is a model for the teacher — to enjoy losing an argument to a student, to recognize his or her contribution, to let the student surpass the teacher.

In the encounter with the teacher who takes you seriously, you learn to take yourself seriously. In the eyes of the one who sees what you can accomplish, you gain a vision of yourself as more than you thought you were. The ideal professor is the one who inspires to dream of what you can be, to try for more than you ever have accomplished before. Everyone who succeeds in life can point to such a teacher, whether in the classroom or on the sports field. It may be a parent, a coach, employer, grade school or high school or art or music teacher. It is always the one who cared enough to criticize, and stayed around to praise.

But what about college professors? To define an ideal for their work, let me offer guidelines on how to treat professors the way we treat students: to give grades.

Professors grade students' work. The conscientious ones spend time reading and thinking about student papers, inscribing their comments and even discussing with students the strengths and weaknesses of their work. But no professor spends as much time on grading students' work as students spend on grading their professors as teachers and as people.

For from the beginning of a course ("Shall I register?") through the middle ("It's boring . . . shall I stick it out?") to the very end ("This was a waste of time"), the students invest time and intellectual energy in deciding what they think, both about how the subject is studied and about the person who presents it. Since effective teaching requires capturing the students' imagination, and since sharp edges and colorful ways excite imagination, the professor who is a "character" is apt, whether liked or disliked, to make a profound impression and perhaps also to leave a mark on the students' minds. The drab professors, not gossiped about and not remembered except for what they taught, may find that even what they taught is forgotten. People in advertising and public relations, politics and merchandising, know that. A generation raised on television expects to be manipulated and entertained.

Yet the emphasis on striking characteristics is irrelevant. Many students have no more sophistication in evaluating professors than they do in evaluating deodorants. This should not be surprising, since they approach them both in the same manner. The one who is "new, different, improved," whether a professor or a bar of soap, wins attention. In this context people have no way of determining good from bad. I once asked an airline pilot, "What is the difference between a good landing and a bad one?" He replied, "A good landing is any landing you can pick yourself up and walk away from." To this pilot, the landing is judged solely by its ultimate goal — safely delivering the plane's passengers. Can we tell when a teacher has safely delivered the student for the next stage of the journey? Can we define the differences between a good teacher and a bad one?

Students have their own definitions of *good* and *bad*, and professors generally have a notion of the meaning of students' grades. Let us consider how students evaluate their teachers, examining in turn the A, B, and C professors. We will begin at the bottom of one scale and work our way up. Let us at the same time consider what kind of student seeks which grade.

Grade C Professors

The first type is the C professor. This is the professor who registers minimum expectations and adheres to the warm-body theory of grading. If a warm body fills a seat regularly and exhibits vital signs, such as breathing at regular intervals, occasionally reading, and turning in some legible writing on paper, then cosmic justice demands, and the professor must supply, the grade of C or *Satisfactory*. The effort needed to achieve F or *No Credit* is considerably greater. One must do no reading, attend few class sessions, and appear to the world to be something very like a corpse.

The professor who, by the present criteria, earns a C respects the students' rights and gives them their money's worth. He or she sells them a used car, so to speak, that they at least can drive off the lot. At the very least the professor does the following:

1. Attends all class sessions, reaches class on time, and ends class at the scheduled hour.
2. Prepares a syllabus for the course and either follows it or revises it, so that students always know what topic is under (even totally confused) discussion.
3. Announces and observes scheduled office hours, so that students have access to the professor without groveling or special pleading, heroic efforts at bird-dogging, or mounting week-long treasure hunts.
4. Makes certain that books assigned for a course are on reserve in the library and sees to it that the bookstore has ample time in which to order enough copies of the textbooks and ancillary reading for a course.
5. Comes to class with a clear educational plan, a well-prepared presentation, a concrete and specific intellectual agenda.
6. Reads examinations with the care invested in them (certainly no more, but also no less)

and supplies intelligible grades and at least
minimal comments; or keeps office hours
for the discussion of the substance of the
examination (but not the grade); and supplies course performance reports — all these
as duty, not acts of grace.

These things constitute student rights. No student has to thank
a professor for doing what he or she is paid to do, and these
six items, at a minimum, are the prerequisites of professional
behavior. They are matters of form, to be sure, but the grade
C is deemed by (some) students to be a matter of good form
alone; the warm-body theory of this grade applies to professors and students alike.

"Tell me my duty and I shall do it" are the words of the
minimally prepared. Just as students of mediocre quality want
to know the requirements and assume that if they meet them,
they have fulfilled their whole obligation to the subject, so
mediocre professors do what they are supposed to do. The subject is in hand; there are no problems. The C professor need
not be entirely bored with the subject, but he or she is not
apt to be deeply engaged by it.

Grade C professors may be entertaining, warm, and loving.
Indeed, many of them must succeed on the basis of personality, because all they have to offer is the studied technology
of attractive personalities. They may achieve huge followings
among the students, keep students at the edge of their seats
with jokes and banter, badger students to retain their interest, but in the end what they have sold, conveyed, or imparted
to the students' minds is themselves, not their mode of thinking or analyzing. Why? Because C professors do not think
much; they rely on the analysis of others.

Above all, the grade C professor has made no effort to take
over and reshape the subject. This person is satisfied with the
mere repetition, accurate and competent repetition to be sure,
of what others have discovered and declared to be true. If
this sort of professor sparks any vitality and interest in students, then he or she will remind students of their better high

school teachers, the people who, at the very least, knew what they were talking about and wanted the students to know. At the end of a course, students should ask themselves, Have I learned facts, or have I grasped how the subject works, its inner dynamic, its logic and structure? If at the end students know merely one fact after another, students should be grateful — at least they have learned that much — but award the professor a polite C. For the professor has done little more than what is necessary.

Grade B Professors

A course constitutes a large and detailed statement on the nature of a small part of a larger subject, a practical judgment upon a particular field of study and how it is to be organized and interpreted. The grade of B is accorded to the student who has mastered the basic and fundamental modes of thought about, and facts contained within, the subject of a course.

The grade B professor is one who can present coherently the larger theory and logic of the subject, who will do more than is required to convey his or her ideas to the students, and who will sincerely hope he or she is inspiring the minds of the students. B professors, as they continue to grow as scholars, are not very different from A professors; they might be described as teachers striving to become A professors. But they are definitely very different from C professors. Let us, then, move on to consider A professors, keeping in mind that B professors will probably become A professors.

Grade A Professors

Grade A professors are the scholar-teachers, a university's prized treasures among a faculty full of intangible riches. America has many faculties of excellence, groups of men and women who with exceptional intelligence take over a subject and make it their own, reshape it and hand it on, wholly changed but essentially unimpaired in tradition, to another generation.

The grade of A goes to student work that attends in some interesting way and with utmost seriousness to the center and whole of the subject of the course. Notice, I did not say that an A goes to the student who says something new and original. That is too much to hope, especially in studying a subject that for hundreds or thousands of years has appeared to the best minds as an intricate and difficult problem.

The grade A professors may have odd ideas about their subjects, but they are asking old-new questions, seeking fresh insight, trying to enter into the way in which the subject works, to uncover its logic and inner structure. What makes an effective high school teacher is confidence, even glibness. What makes an effective university teacher is doubt and dismay. The scholarly mind is marked by self-criticism and thirsty search; it is guided by an awareness of its own limitations and those of knowledge. The scholar-teacher, of whatever subject or discipline, teaches one thing: Knowledge is not sure but uncertain, scholarship is search, and to teach is to impart the lessons of doubt. What is taught is what we do not know.

On whom do you bestow a grade A? It is given to the professor who, stumbling and falling, yet again rising up and walking on, seeks both knowledge and the meaning of knowledge. It is to the one who always asks, *Why* am I telling you these things? Why should you know them? It is to the professor who demands ultimate seriousness for his or her subject because the subject must be known, who not only teaches but professes, stands for, represents, the thing taught. The grade A professor lives for the subject, needs to tell you about it, wants to share it. The Nobel Prize scientist who so loved biology that she gave her life to it even without encouragement and recognition for a half a century of work, the literary critic who thinks getting inside a poem is entering Paradise, the historian who assumes the human issues of the thirteenth century live today — these exemplify the ones who are ultimately serious about a subject.

One who has made this commitment to a field of scholarship can be readily identified. This is the one full of concern, the one who commits upon the facts the act of advocacy, who deems compelling what others find merely interesting. The scholar-teacher is such because he or she conveys the self-evident, the obvious fact that facts bear meaning, constituting a whole that transcends the sum of the parts. True, to the world this sense of ultimate engagement with what is merely interesting or useful information marks the professor as demented, as are all those who march to a different drummer. What I mean to say is simple. Anybody who cares so much about what to the rest of the world is so little must be a bit daft. Why should such things matter so much — why, above all, things of the mind or the soul or the heart, things of nature and mathematics, things of structure and weight and stress, things of technology and science, society and mind? Professors often remember lonely childhoods (for my part, I don't). As adults, too, professors have to spend long hours by themselves in their offices, reading books, or in their laboratories or at their computers, or just thinking all by themselves. That is not ordinary and commonplace behavior. This is what it means to march to a different drummer. A student earns an A when he or she has mastered the larger theory of the course, entered into its logic and meaning, discovered a different way of seeing. Like a professor, the student who through accurate facts and careful, critical thought seeks meaning, the core and center of the subject, earns the grade A.

Yet matters cannot be left here. I do not mean to promote advocacy for its own sake. Students have rights too, and one of these is the right to be left alone, to grow and mature in their own distinctive ways. They have the right to seek their way, just as we professors find ours. The imperial intellect, the one that cannot allow autonomy, is a missionary, not a teacher. Many compare the imperial teacher with the A professor, but if you look closely at their different ways of teaching, you will see that this is an error. The teacher leads, says, "Follow me," without looking backward. The missionary pushes, imposes self upon another autonomous self. This is the opposite of teaching, and bears no relevance to learning or to scholarship. The teacher persuades; the missionary preaches. The teacher argues; the missionary shouts others to silence. The teacher wants the student to discover; the missionary decides what the student must discover. The teacher enters class with fear and trembling, not knowing where the discussion will lead. The missionary knows at the start of a class exactly what the students must cover by the end of the class.

Grade A professors teach, never indoctrinate. They educate rather than train. There is a fine line to be drawn, an invisible boundary, between great teaching and self-aggrandizing indoctrination.

Knowledge and even understanding do not bring salvation and therefore do not have to be, and should not be, forced upon another. And this brings me back to the earlier emphasis upon scholarship as the recognition of ignorance, the awareness not of what we know but of how we know and of what we do not know. The true scholar, who also is the true teacher, is drawn by self-criticism, compelled by doubting, skeptical curiosity, knows the limits of knowing. He or she cannot be confused with the imperial, the arrogant, and the proselytizing. By definition, we stand for humility before the unknown.

A good professor wants to answer the question, Why am I telling you these things? A good student wants to answer the question, Why am I taking these courses? What do I hope to get out of them? Why are they important to me? I have not put before you any unattainable ideals in these questions. Some of us realize them every day, and nearly all of us realize them on some days. Just as students' transcripts rarely present only A's or *No Credits*, so professors rarely succeed all of the time. No one bears the indelible grade of A.

Chapter Four

The Apprenticeship
of the Mind

CHOLARSHIP IS THE SYSTEMATIC AND rigorous study of a subject or a problem. The scholar creates a fresh reading of the subject, a distinctive approach to a problem. Whether the scholar publishes or transmits discoveries in other media does not matter. What is important is that the scholar takes up in a new and interesting way a long-standing problem, on the one side, or a long-familiar, yet ever-interesting text, on the other. Ideally, education should introduce students to this process of learning, enabling them to discover that learning is a process that goes on in their teachers' minds as well as in their own minds. For all of us solve problems and see things new. What we do in academic scholarship, in the security of the study and the laboratory, is use our minds to think strictly, clearly, and sharply. And this is the quality of thought that enhances every life that rises above the mechanical. It is this process of thought that is one of the goals of all education.

Scholarship, as distinguished from education, cannot take place in the large classroom. Works of scholarship, like works of art, cannot be mass-produced. For fresh work is work that progresses thoughtfully, in an unlimited exploration. Students must listen and be listened to, professors must not merely report but explain their mode of thought. There must be conversation, and people must work at dialogue. Yet dialogue is difficult among more than two dozen students. This presents a dilemma for the student who wants to feel his or her mind develop fully. Small liberal arts colleges present an ideal setting for teaching: small classes, warm community, shared values. But scholars need an environment that small liberal arts colleges cannot provide, such as first-rate libraries and excellent laboratories. As a result, scholars tend to pursue their work at great state universities and at large rich private universities — where there are large classes and students listen to the professor's lectures, but study with graduate students. For the student this means an adequate exposure to a subject area and its basic material, but the graduate student may not be able to offer more than that. The student will be well informed about the subject, but will miss the deeper understanding of the professor who is also a scholar.

What is missing in the graduate student or lesser professor is a quality of mind that will spark the same quality in the student. To develop this distinctive quality of mind is the continuing task of those engaged in the nurturing of future scholars. Four traits characterize the mind of the scholar, young or old, freshman or senior, beginning or experienced, academic or nonacademic, and none of them can be taught, only exemplified. The first is the desire to rethink important propositions and to ask how they work and why we have been compelled to accede to them. The second is the capacity to take important intellectual initiatives, to ask questions in addition to accepting answers, to want to know not only more about what is known but also about something others have never asked. The third is the complete engagement with the work, the entire devotion to the task to the exclusion of all else, more simply the ability to concentrate. The fourth is love for the work, a love that means finding the full meaning of life in what one is doing.

Any one of these traits without the others yields not the scholar but the dilettante: a politician of ideas, a dealer in manufactured and available notions, an amateur with bright ideas. Without these four traits, the intelligence never reaches its full potential of being more than a skill, a basic ability.

Let me name a few scholars who thought the unthinkable — and prevailed. First, there was Charles Darwin. Second, there was Sigmund Freud. Third, there was Copernicus. In the worlds of nature, mind, and the universe, these three pioneers exemplify the power of the scholar to ask the unthinkable questions, to reexamine the basic questions everyone assumes have been answered. These men and women like Madame Curie typify in their work the process of scholarship. Darwin allowed his careful observations to lead him to conclusions that defied long-established facts. Freud insisted on taking seriously phenomena people insisted bore no meaning at all. Copernicus explained old facts in a completely new way. The first one worked inductively, the second reasoned independently, and the third thought courageously, seeing as fresh so-called facts everybody had accepted. These are the heroes of scholarship, and we do in our lives what they did in their work. We do it not only as scholars but also as reflective citizens, children and parents, husbands and wives — we use the fullness of our minds in all manner of relationships and all manner of work.

Education takes two forms, and both are necessary for scholarship. The first is the acquisition of knowledge, of facts and their understanding. The second is an apprenticeship to those who teach the work by doing it. All undergraduates are well served by great professors, people who teach what is known in a responsible and conscientious way. Some students will experience an apprenticeship as well. I can give three common examples of the master-apprentice relationship that most of us will recognize and have perhaps experienced. First, in music school, the teacher plays, the student imitates — and tries to play better. Second, the sports field, the coach demonstrates, the athlete copies — and does it better. Third, students copy a parent, on the one side, and a teacher on the other, but they improve on much.

The apprenticeship offers the student an opportunity that cannot be duplicated in a lecture class. There is no simple way to show someone how to take intellectual initiative: how to ask questions, how to draw analogies from the known to the unknown, from the completed to the unattempted. Under ideal conditions, professors aspire to exemplify — or, more honestly, adumbrate — the things we try to be. We educate our students by example as much as by word. We cast our shadow on the wall for the disciples to see. For what students see in their teachers is related to the model of what they want to be. We may present an attractive or an unattractive model, but always a choice.

The apprentice learns the craft by imitating it. They know success when what they make surpasses what the artisan has made, for the artisan strives to teach the apprentice to transcend the limits of the artisan's abilities. For some students education will achieve the goal of the artisan, nurturing a mind that can see farther and sharper than the teacher's. The setting for this form of education is not so much the classroom as the study, not the place where results of research are announced but the laboratory and library where the discoveries are made. The setting is wherever there is a beginning. It is the place of inquiry, discovery, by doing for oneself, by finding out for oneself.

Research is what a person does when he or she undertakes to test established truths. Research is what a person does when he or she proposes to find out whether what people take for granted is fact. Research is what someone does who asks, What if . . . ? and Why . . . ? and Why not . . . ? Must professors supervise research? No, though they can help. Can freshmen undertake research? Most certainly, if they want to try. Research is not merely learning about an obscure subject closed to the vast majority of people. That is mere erudition, fact mongering. Research can occur anywhere; it is defined only by an attitude of mind and heart, of inquiry and stubbornness, of care and attentiveness, of clarity of thought and even originality. Many learned people can teach, but only the scholarly mind can nurture other scholars. Only the person who knows how to undertake the search can show others how to do so. Only the scholar, like the artisan, can teach by example so that others may learn by doing.

Scholars never cease to be students and disciples, never cease to learn, and those who are beginners in our craft never serve only as students and disciples until the day they formally become scholars. We are always learners as well as teachers. So, too, even beginners should take up tasks of scholarship, while still acquiring the requisite knowledge and skills. We learn by doing. And while doing, we always learn. We cannot postpone the work of doing until we have learned all we think we need to know, for we will never know all we need in order to do what we want to do. When students begin their studies, therefore, they ought to find themselves plunged into an ongoing seminar, a kind of laboratory for research into a common problem by individuals working together, from different angles and on different data. All can benefit to varying degrees, and those who can benefit most should receive nothing less.

Let me give an example that will be familiar to students at many colleges and universities: the seminar. What is a seminar? It is a course in which professors do not lecture. Rather, participants — students — present their ideas to one another. They write their papers under the professor's guidance, but the papers are their own. They read their papers to their fellow students and gain the benefit of their comments and criticism. A well-constructed seminar will present a single complex problem for collective study. Individual members of the seminar will take a part of the larger problem and write papers about it. All together, the group discusses the problem as a whole, with each student contributing his or her share. A seminar on the causes of the American Revolution, for example, would present a dozen students pursuing a dozen proposed causes, advocating and analyzing the character and place of each. Taken together, the individual student contributions would produce a coherent picture. Most colleges and universities offer seminars at the upper levels of the curriculum, usually for seniors. Some offer seminars for freshmen as well. A seminar offers no easy answers to a problem through lecture notes, and the student is forced to think independently about a difficult question. It is at this point that learning takes place.

The seminar requires the student to cross a crucial threshold. The most difficult thing for a scholar to learn is to learn from other people, to preserve an open mind to the ideas and insight, even to the questions and scholarly programs, shaped by coworkers. In the seminar the student learns to respect the criticism and ideas of other students, and to recognize the limits on his or her own perceptions. Because scholarship requires single-mindedness and dedication, scholars face the temptation to dismiss as unimportant the questions and inquiries of others. It is not because we are committed, but because those questions are distracting. This attitude of self-sufficiency, this incapacity to learn from others except what one needs for the particular task at hand, closes the path to scholarship.

Professors are responsible for teaching the lessons that we do learn from others. We always carry on our work alongside that of our colleagues, and often with their help, and we must learn to listen to and consider fairly the concerns and problems of others, colleagues and noncolleagues alike. If students learn that what they need from others is not approval but insight, then we have opened the way to great achievement.

This observation leads to a difficult question: How do we as professors measure the success of our work in education? It is, alas, a measure that we are not in a position to take: the total mode of life adopted by our students. If we succeed, we open the doors of learning, the world of the mind, to the coming generations. Our young apprentices go forth, and some will carry on the work of the teacher, knowing something about teaching and much about the self-conscious and articulated requirements of learning. The new craftsmen, having turned the wheel ten thousand times, will still wonder at the potentialities of the wheel, the clay, the pot, and the hands. And if we fail, then we foist upon the coming generations a mass of closed-minded, self-important careerists, people who impose dogma and recite facts.

My own ideal is for my work to be made obsolete, of mere historic interest, by the greater achievements of my apprentices. Among my doctoral students of years past several have surpassed me in the areas in which they work. One of them has undertaken exceptional research. Another has taken over and mastered an area of research I left behind, and his work now far surpasses mine. A third went on to problems of thought and theory that lay beyond the range of my ability. That is what I mean by having students who learn from but then surpass the teacher. This is the only way I know to transcend self and to surpass my own limitations. The formidable obstacles to us all, teachers and students alike, are those of the spirit and the flesh, the challenge of tough and intractable clay, infirm and unskilled hands, a wheel on a wobbly pivot, and the pot none before has ever imagined, or yet made — the one each of us dreams about.

Chapter Five

The New Humanities and the Old Academy

HE REVOLUTION OF THE 1960s AND 1970s brought to the campus a whole new set of subjects — along with new groups of people to study and teach them. The history of women, blacks, Jews, Asian-Americans, Polish-Americans, Chicanos, and other groups joined the established curriculum of English, American, and Western European studies.

During those two decades students brought about fundamental change by demanding that studies relate to everyday life; students insisted on "relevance." The meaning of the word relevance proved unclear, but students insisted. They wanted to know why they were studying the subjects at hand. They asked what the curriculum had to do with them as people, with their lives and their futures. The question of relevance produced diverse answers. Here I want to deal with the answer that has made the greatest difference: the interest in subjects regarded as relevant to those who differed from typical white male students — women, blacks, Jews, Catholics, the Greek Orthodox, Hispanics, Asian-Americans. These students wanted to study books important to them as Jews, Catholics, and so on. As a result of the demand for relevance, programs, centers, and departments of Judaic, Afro-American, and women's studies (among other fields) were organized. These new subjects confront students today, and they have vastly enlarged the college curriculum everywhere.

In the course catalog today, college students find an account of whole sectors of American society that earlier generations of college students will not have known, or they will find subjects that earlier generations would have regarded as a private and personal realm. That is, if you are male, white, Protestant, of northern and western European or old American parentage, you will wonder why you should consider a course in the black experience in the Caribbean, the formation of Judaism in Talmudic times, the Roman Catholic renaissance of the eighteenth century, or women in American history (a course my son took, with enormously broadening results, in his senior year in high school). But if you are Roman Catholic, or Greek Orthodox, or black, or Hispanic, or a woman, you will find a place for yourself in the curriculum that is offered to all students equally. And this place in the curriculum is testimony that your special experience matters to the life of the college. That is one great achievement of the cultural revolution.

The revolution in the 1960s and early 1970s brought about a considerable expansion of the established curriculum of humanistic learning in American and Canadian universities. Departments of history that formerly concentrated American and Western European history made room for regions formerly ignored, such as Asia or sub-Saharan Africa. Departments of literature that were formerly interested in only English, American, French, German, and Russian literature began to ask students to read Afro-American and Latin American literature. For me, the single most dramatic development of the 1960s proved to be the opening of the study of religion to encompass traditions and religious communities beyond Christianity: first and foremost, Judaism. In these and other ways, therefore, the humanistic disciplines paid attention to the history, literature, and religion of groups formerly assumed to have none worth studying.

If we ask ourselves why at just that time, university humanists discovered an importance in subjects formerly not recognized at all, we may point to three factors. First, in the 1950s, America had assumed a preeminent position in world affairs, with the result that Americans began to take an interest in parts of the world formerly beyond the horizon.

Accordingly, Russian studies were born, and concurrently the conception of area studies took shape. An area or region such as the Soviet Union, or the Near and Middle East, or North Africa, might provide the focus for diverse disciplines and their practitioners: historians, literary specialists, not to mention anthropologists, geographers, sociologists, political scientists, scholars of religions. After the iron grip of the established areas and regions — Western Europe mainly, America secondarily — was loosened, area studies would encompass the whole of human civilization. Indeed, the first important break with convention lay in the establishment of American studies as a recognized field not only of literature and history but of everything else. American studies expanded to include social history, the economy, folklore and folk life, archaeology, anthropology, the Afro-American experience, native American studies — a vast range of topics, beyond the established and conventional ones. All of them constituted facts about a single area, a given region. Once the field of American studies was established, the principle of area studies as a subject was established, and a wide range of area studies programs could follow. Moreover, now that the universities had made a place for regional studies, it would be difficult to include one region while excluding another.

The second reason for the new inclusiveness is that groups whose opinions were formerly submerged or ignored now appeared in college classes. Whether constituted as a group by race, ethnic origin, religion, or sex, these groups wished to make their presence felt in higher education. Most could not state exactly what that ought to mean. But they knew they did not wish any longer to be ignored, treated as though they were invisible. Who were they? Jews and Catholics, then blacks, Puerto Ricans and "other Hispanics," Asian-Americans, American Indians, not to mention Scandinavians, Italians and Poles, and women — the list is long and varied. The members of the list shared the aspiration to enter the academic curriculum. But with the enormous diversification of the constituency of universities, with Jews no longer carefully counted one by one and instructed not to count at all, with blacks no longer completely isolated, with other groups no longer forgotten, with women no longer merely tolerated so long as they acted as men wanted them to, universities clearly had to change. They had to accept fundamental changes already taking place in the character of American society and culture, and they did. The curriculum of a university, whatever else it does, serves as an enormously effective statement on what matters and what does not matter in America.

These two factors — a change in the nation's politics and a shift in the nation's list of recognized groups — joined with yet a third to produce the changes I have characterized as the birth of the new humanities. That third factor affected the universities alone. It consisted of the effects of the tidal wave of growth that followed the arrival of the baby boom generation on campus. Not only was the generation coming of age in the 1960s much larger than any before it, but a higher proportion of young people chose to go on to college. The size of this college generation imposed an enormous burden by forcing old universities to expand and by leading other educators to found new universities, colleges, community colleges, and the like. What followed in the age of unprecedented expansion should have surprised no one. New teachers had to be hired. These teachers could no longer be drawn only from protected castes — the "Anglo-Saxons" and those who acted like them. As women demanded recognition in the curriculum, so some women found a place, also, in faculties, as did Jews in numbers unthinkable a generation earlier, Catholics, once no more welcome than Jews, and pretty much anybody who could present appropriate credentials. The homogeneity of old American universities, with their old American faculties and their old American names and genealogies, quickly disappeared.

Once universities had opened their doors to larger and more diverse social and ethnic constituencies than they had ever known, the question confronted faculties and students alike: What do we do now? The answer was simply to do more than had been done before. This meant that students could study what was familiar in their own background. Relevance became a criterion. But this was both natural and normal, and just as students had always done. The old Americans had always known what was relevant to them: Classics, after all, was a gentleman's hobby, English literature belonged to the descendants of English immigrants, and American history was the history written by the old Americans' great-grandfathers. A certain snobbery, of course, protected these scheduled subjects; people absorbed the prejudice that, quite naturally and predictably, these were things *any* educated person should know. Knowing these subjects, or this list of selected books (the one hundred books for the one hundred families that count), or that knowledge, defined education. Hence a core curriculum and a general education was possible. No one needed to ask about the excluded hundreds of thousands of books, classics to the excluded groups, and the millions of excluded families, from which students now came. Before the 1960s, everybody knew what was what: what was worthwhile and represented taste, what shaped thoughts worth thinking, what defined values worth adopting. And it should be added, people who knew these worthwhile things also could look forward to careers of worth and standing: in banks, law firms, corporations, hospitals, universities, and other protected professions reserved for those who came from the right castes and knew the scheduled subjects.

All that had to change, and it has changed. But no one has yet reckoned with how to take hold of the change and make sense of it. For the change proved not entirely for the good. What seemed relevant to one proved remote to the next. The curriculum came to resemble the ethnic politics of large industrial states in the 1920s and 1930s, with a slice of the pie for everyone, but no sense of a common good or a public interest. This only emphasized the apparent differences between the new and the old humanities. The old humanities had preserved not only privilege but also a center, a sense of purpose. Their imperial view did encompass everybody, for the old humanists imagined that they had something to say to the whole of humanity and that what they had to say demanded a universal audience. Teachers of the established humanities could indeed point to books they believed everyone should read. *And they could say why.* These teachers could also define traits of intellectual excellence and, again, say why they were so defined. A teacher of the old humanities, therefore, could imagine such a thing as a general education. So, they held, people could determine why one book mattered more than another, and why one philosophical tradition deserved close and careful scrutiny while another preserved mere gibberish. The power of the conventional and established humanities lay in the promise of educated taste and reasoned judgment. The old humanities promised to impose order upon the chaos of information, to sort through and to select the books and ideas that truly nurtured character and culture.

Against this intellectual order and serenity pressed the motley crowd of the new humanities. What did the new humanities offer to justify their entry into the realm of the disciplined intellect? The mere presence of a new sort of human being, formerly excluded, hardly constituted a persuasive argument. After all, that new person, whether black, Catholic, woman, or Jew, could readily study the classics of the established curriculum and adopt its values. Generations of "minorities" had done so. But what universally accessible human experience did the new constituencies bring to the campus, to challenge the classics of human intellect that, all together, had constituted the old humanities? Where was the Jewish Aquinas or the Indian Plato, the black Shakespeare, the Catholic equivalent to the Reformation that everyone studies with such admiration? Many were ready to answer these questions. But when the new humanities pointed to their heritage of art, music, fiction, and poetry, few but those to whom it was relevant were prepared to look. People took for granted, both old and new alike, that the blacks would come. And after considering, they made another assumption. Blacks would study what blacks had done. Jews would study Jewish studies. Women would study women's studies. What this meant in practice was that most students in Jewish studies courses were Jews, most students in Afro-American studies courses were blacks, and most students in women's studies courses were women. (In my own case I found that it took many years before the profile of students in my basic courses matched the profile of Brown students in general, so that non-Jewish students found it perfectly routine to take a course with me.) But then they made one more assumption. Everyone would still study the familiar philosophy, the Shakespeare, the Reformation, that everyone had always studied, in the ways in which everyone had always studied them.

So was formed the benign consensus of the 1970s: insiders teaching private subjects to insiders, and everyone learning public subjects as they had always been taught. Everyone for a time accepted the compromise. The newcomers felt quite at home, as well they should, for they never left their ghettos. What this meant for students was that Jewish students took for granted they could get easy A's in Jewish studies courses — and please their parents too. Black students insisted that only blacks could teach, and study, Afro-American subjects. The new humanities remained on the fringes of the real interests of students at large. What the new humanities might teach — the great human experiences of the black peoples in America and Africa, the remarkable record of service and of suffering of Israel, the Jewish people then and now, for instance — never enriched the curriculum. The established humanities retained their ultimate governance. Making room for newcomers, the old humanities remained essentially unchanged. The old privileges endured and did not even have to be shared. What emerged, then, through the 1970s was curricular tokenism, a kind of intellectual affirmative action: There were black women receptionists and clever Jews in the research department, but the board of directors would come from the same good folk who had supplied members for generations past. Everyone would be contented.

Not surprisingly, the easy compromise of the 1970s has broken down. The new humanities cannot sustain themselves if they address only special interests. The established humanities cannot explain themselves any longer. The newcomers have proved inadequate to the tasks and the old-timers have fallen into bankruptcy. How so? The new humanities, in their dominant form, made no important claim upon the university. They consist of Jews teaching Jewish things to Jews, and blacks to blacks, and women to women. But universities should be places where everybody speaks to whoever is interested. Scholars speak to everybody about truth and matters of scholarship and interpretation. No one talks to himself alone or speaks of experience inaccessible to all or demands assent to a view others cannot grasp within a common logic. Accordingly, the formal distinction between insider and outsider, upon which the new humanities have built, finds no place among the foundations of universities.

The new humanities, moreover, have not had much to say to the community at large. They offer no reasoned response to the argument that some things matter more than others, white things more than black, Aquinas more than Maimonides, the Old Testament as Protestants read it more than Scripture and tradition as Catholics know them or as "the whole Torah of Moses, our rabbi," as Jews revere it. Once the new humanities conceded that theirs was an essentially private and particular heritage, to be promoted for parochial purposes (to give blacks self-confidence, to persuade Jews to remain Jewish), they also turned themselves into mere pressure groups on the campus, extensions of political forces based outside the campus.

The result for black studies has proved disastrous. James Lardner reports, in *The Washington Post,* that in the late 1960s and early 1970s, there were more than 500 formal programs in black or Afro-American studies. By late 1982 only 275 programs survived; of these, only 65 or 70 were full departments. Scholars of black studies concede that their field has entered "a state of near-crisis." Why? Because the black students themselves avoid black studies. The scholars excuse themselves by explaining that the students are "more job-conscious and more interested in courses that will make them employable." This is pure self-indulgence. In this same period classics has enjoyed a renaissance, although few jobs these days demand knowledge of Attic Greek or the ability to read Plato in the original. Anyone who doubts that the same story may be told of Jewish studies and other ethnic studies needs only to attend a meeting of the learned societies of those fields. Gone is the atmosphere of hope and energy.

Newer subjects also give evidence of regression. The academic study of religion, which was born in the later 1940s and fully realized in the 1960s as part of the larger development under discussion here, is old and feeble. At a recent national meeting, the scholars held a caucus of "endangered departments." One participant guessed, "Every religion department from Springfield, Missouri, to the tip of Maine is endangered, whether the department chairmen know it or not." The simple fact is that people take for granted that a university can exist without black, Jewish, women's, or religious studies, but a university cannot exist without history, English, philosophy, or sociology.

What went wrong? The new humanities have not yet taken the measure of universities; universities have not yet imparted their distinctive character to the new humanities. That is one fact, with two complementary effects. The new humanities have a future in universities only if they join the sort of discourse that universities nurture. The university, for its part, must build its future upon the broadest social foundations and draw upon the deepest cultural resources of human experience and culture. And that can happen only when the university demonstrates, as it has not yet shown, the universal power of its program of inquiry to illuminate the analysis of human experience across the globe, to make interesting and public what is at present self-serving and private. Each side, whether the new or the old, the outsider or the one at home, bears part of the responsibility for the reform of the new humanities. Professors of the new subjects will have to demonstrate how the things they know contribute to a common inquiry and a shared conversation. They must cease to turn away from their colleagues and to assume they address a protected audience within a privileged sanctuary — as though they could not compete for attention. Professors of the established subjects will have to open their minds to areas of learning they have, to date, treated with unjustified disdain and ignorant indifference. Both sides are accomplices in the easy compromise, which has perpetuated privilege and merely expanded its range.

The only issue in the rise and fall of the old and new humanities is scholarship. Scholarship by its nature pays no heed to special claims. A proposition that one cannot understand unless qualified by gifts of genealogy or social standing gains no hearing at all. A course on a subject only Jews can understand will not endure and in the end will attract no Jews. A book that speaks to people only if they believe at the outset that the book is true or important will enjoy a long life on the library shelf. The binding will never suffer endless opening and closings. Such a book is a mere curiosity.

Such books, such courses, in the end go the way of all claims at reaching judgments through other than critical and reasonable modes of thought. They enjoy the fate of every truth that is known *a priori*, rather than through inductive inquiry and testing, every conviction that is exempt from verification and falsification. Scholarship as we practice it is inductive; it aims at falsifying or verifying all claims to truth, and subjects all propositions to the same critical and reasonable modes of thought. When universities treat ethnic studies as special, when practitioners of those studies claim they can be appreciated only by members of their own group, then scholarship ceases. In the beginning, the new humanities flourished by presenting surprising information about subjects no one cared to study. Playing an endless game of show and tell, justified by self-indulgent special pleading, the professors of the new humanities gathered everything but a reason for their field. For their part, the universities proposed to accommodate what in fact most people despised and would dismiss as soon as they decently could. For universities are not museums, and professors mean to add to knowledge, not only preserve and display it. The first phase in the new humanities has proved deeply flawed: arrival without welcome, presence without purpose.

Since universities are nurtured by the societies that sponsor them and the politics that give effect to social policy, universities will hardly benefit from reverting to the earlier world of institutionalized prejudice and cultural snobbery. American society will never tolerate the reintroduction of quotas to exlude Jews, let alone the implementation of the bigotry that blacks cannot learn and women should not. In the same way, the new humanities will fail the universities and society if they continue to exclude the larger intellectual community. Black history must be open to the work of white scholars, and women's studies must allow men to read, write, and evaluate. The task of the new humanities is to gain legitimate entry into the intellectual life of the universities. The task of the universities is to draw from every group within its boundaries the same principles of reasoned discourse and public accounting of all propositions that have framed scholarship and defined worthwhile learning. Both parties must now move on from the initial uneasy accommodation.

How shall we achieve the integration of the new humanities within the university's conception of its own work? To begin with, let me state what I do: *I teach students.* And what I teach to students is about Judaism — in that order. What we teach students, through any subject, is about thinking, about using their minds for specific tasks. The curriculum then consists of two components: first, information, which students learn, and, second, an example of how we compose that information into intelligible propositions, arguments about possibilities, which students may choose to imitate and improve. Whether we teach undergraduates or graduate students, the issue is the same. Students should be concerned with modes of analysis and means of interpretation, through which they learn the particulars of information. When we impart information without articulating how we have formulated the specifics and worked out the details in one way rather than another, we do only part of our work, the part, alas, most rapidly forgotten or rendered obsolete. In the words of my coworker William Scott Green, of the University of Rochester, "Teaching means to teach students how to do something, how to know something, how to understand something."

By this criterion, one subject serves as well as any other, the history of the Jews as much as the history of the ancient Romans or the medieval French or the modern Americans, the literature of the American blacks as much as the literature of the English, the religious world of Islam as much as that of Christianity, the Roman Catholic experience of Christianity as much as the Protestant. For whatever we teach stands or falls by the same criterion: Does the subject at hand present the possibility of analyzing generally intelligible propositions? Does the area of learning generate theses worth sustained testing, ideas capable of providing insight beyond themselves and transcending the limits of the world that gave them first light? To accord to white male experience the status of the norm and to black or female experience the status of the abnormal, then, is no longer a valid proposition. For human experience properly described, analyzed, and interpreted speaks to us all. But without analysis and argument, no experience *self-evidently* establishes the norm (or diverges from it).

Accordingly, universities engaged in scholarship do more than simply accommodate the new humanities. Colleges can no longer imagine scholarship in ignorance of the corpus of human experience and achievement taken up in those new humanities. Rigorous thought about what matters must by definition focus on black as much as white, just as biology inquires into the blood of anyone. The very nature of the disciplines and of the discourse of university scholarship requires the full recognition of the new humanities alongside the established ones. Why? Because we cannot do our work without them all.

How shall we who represent the new groups — women, blacks, Jews, Hispanics — proceed? In my view the task falls upon the shoulders of the new humanities. If we claim right of entry, ours is the burden of presenting a valid ticket of admission. We professors have to teach everyone equally. And we must first teach students to broaden their sympathies. The books people wrote in the submerged and ignored sectors of humanity, those of the "wrong" religion, race, sex, part of the world, have won our place for us. Ours — professors and students alike — is the task to ask what do we know about our experience that will speak to the heart and mind of others.

The answer to that question will emerge in our answers to other questions. How do we all exemplify a common experience of humanity? What can we share with outsiders? When we see the ways in which we are like others, and the way in which we are not like others, then we may speak intelligibly and claim a full and solemn hearing for ourselves.

Chapter Six

What the Revolution in Education Accomplished

A New Perspective on the Humanities

 ODAY WE STAND NEARER THE TRUE goals of education than we did before the events of the 1960s and 1970s. A lasting change of those revolutionary years is a change in attitude, a change in the heart and mind of scholars. This is the change that will affect you most deeply as a student, for it will affect what you are taught and how you are taught. The significant change in attitude concerns the humanities and their new definition. You learned in the last chapter that the revolution of the 1960s brought new studies to the university. The appearance of these subjects has forced many — teachers and students alike — to grapple with the concept of the humanities. If you think you are too young to worry about this debate, you are wrong. As soon as you have registered for one course or another you have chosen a side in the debate. This chapter is to help you make a wise choice in your efforts to define the humanities.

People know what sciences teach, and in general they also can make sense of economics or sociology or political science or the other social sciences. But one of the principal components of education in colleges and universities, the humanities, remains elusive. Like many students before you, you will find yourself asking, What do people do in "the humanities"? That is, what do they do in the study of literature, philosophy, languages, music, art, religion, and related subject and disciplines? The question demands an answer, simply because every college student faces requirements not only in practical subjects like natural sciences, social sciences, computers, and mathematics but also in the subjects of history, literature, philosophy, music, art, theater, and the like. These, all together, sail under the flag of humanistic learning. At the outset let us say what the humanities are not. First, they are not "humanitarian," meaning, being nice to people. Second, they are not "humanistic," in the sense of secular and not religious.

Can the humanities be defined by a specific intellectual goal? No. Clear thinking, lucid and simple expression, cogent and connected argument, characterize intellectual power wherever it is found. If some sociologists write jargon and anthropologists talk like barbarians, other sociologists give us classics of insight and other anthropologists create literature of enduring human interest. Medicine, engineering, physics, mathematics, all with their languages and technical vocabulary, conduct their business through clear thought and cogent argument. You can expect at the very least to develop your intellectual power. Beyond that you encounter the specifics of the individual field. Each discipline and field has its own standards of elegance and good argument. A biology student who does not learn how to analyze clearly and to think critically through a problem of interpretation will not do better in English or philosophy (except that the thing studied may more firmly seize his or her imagination).

Is there a standard body of knowledge you can look for? There is no common core of facts that everyone, everywhere, must know, and that we in the humanities in particular teach. The age of imperialism ended a decade ago, and with it died imperialist theories of the mind. Nothing is more "classic" than something else. No book, painting, symphony, sequence of events — known in English as "history" — involving a particular people, no philosophy, language, or religion sustains a contrary claim. All things are subject to taste and critical judgment. All the peoples of humanity now are the subjects of the humanities.

Yet we still teach Shakespeare in preference to doggerel, look at Rembrandt, not graffiti, pay more attention to Christianity, Judaism, or Buddhism than to the ephemera of tarot cards, and think about mind, metaphysics, and ethics, rather than the philosophy of transient matters. There exists a new classicism — the application of taste and judgment.

This definition of a new classicism raises some obvious questions. What are the criteria of taste and critical judgment? Why these criteria and not some others? Asked in this way, the question yields yet another: What is the value of the books you or another chooses to read? What can be classic at this moment of acute contemporaneity? What have the humanities to offer as their distinctive contribution? In the humanities, the intellect common to us all focuses upon a specific aspect of our being, which is our imagination and sensibility, our capacity to appreciate and accordingly to respond to the being of humanity, its existential context. Let me say this in another way. What we teach, that thing which sets us apart, is a work of imagination. It is an artifact of sensibility capable of both exemplifying and allowing access to the unmeasured capacities of humanity to be: to laugh and cry, to feel pain and joy, to hope and endure, so to be as to surpass what we are.

The intellect is common to us all. The use of intellect for the discovery of what we may become is the work of humanistic study. For what humanists study is the potentialities of imagination, in history, philosophy, and literature. For these disciplines explore the great works of imagination and passion (not alone of intellect) and allow us to experience, in the deeds and visions of other men and women, those hitherto unimagined thoughts, unseen visions, unheard sounds, and unplumbed depths of mature emotion, by which we may measure and shape our own capacity. In this way we may transcend our small and limited selves.

If you have qualms about this definition of the humanities, you are probably not alone. I did not always see things this way. Coming from that old and rich tradition of Judaism and of Talmud, I thought all things devolved upon the rational intellect, and what mattered most in humanity was mind. But a colleague persisted in asking, Where in your scheme of education is there room for imagination? To feel with Othello, to weep with Achilles, to admire the heroism and be awed at the nobility of Socrates in the Phaedo? As I grew older and endured difficult times, I experienced genuine suffering, disloyalty, ingratitude. I suffered contempt and rejection from students who learned deeply from me and from colleagues to whose careers I had been devoted. I learned to appreciate the experiences of the heart and I began to reflect upon what there is to be learned about feeling and emotion, as much as reason. In many ways this book became possible only because of what I learned in those difficult years when I got the opposite of what I thought I deserved. For then I had to think long and hard about what I truly believed to be the worth of life, the value of education, the truth of scholarship. I have come to understand that not all the world is mathematics — that (to me) highest achievement of the intellect — nor is reality contained solely by the perception, beneath the accidents of the world, of the enduring patterns of relationship and relation.

The Book of Job is not an essay on the problem of evil, but a work of surpassing art, because therein is the problem of evil made human and accessible to the heart. Behind the dense abstraction of the great German philosopher Immanuel Kant is the urgent problem of the limits of knowledge and the reach of faith and feeling. This one person, at this one place, thought more deeply than had any before him about mind and belief and sentiment and, in a compelling way, their complexities. So too are the eye and the ear to be shown what there is to see and hear. In music and in art we discover how blind and deaf we have been, how much there is to be learned about seeing and hearing — and about the structure to be sought through sight and sound — from the better eyes and ears of others.

But in the enhancement of our capacities to imagine, to transcend ourselves and enter into the being of others, I think the beginning lies in the imagination of potentialities of emotion and sentiment. For not all will ever see or hear or think about thought, but everyone has sentiment and heart. All love and are loved, bury and are buried. None ever passed through life without that, the experience of love and death.

Since the educational revolution of the 1960s, there has been no common core of facts that everyone everywhere must know and that we in particular teach. Nor is there a distinctive grace of intellect that is ours alone. All we have to offer is a particular access: to those moments in history of significant humanness; to those powerful minds in philosophy of transcendent self-awareness; to those sensibilities in literature; and to those anguished, searching hearts in religions in which we may perceive not what we are but what we too can be. This is another kind of classicism, the conviction, which is the value we espouse and profess, that greatness inheres in humanity — that it is worth being human. By the exercise of catholic taste and critical judgment you may make choices among works of human greatness of mind and emotion. Through the selection of what your frail judgment tells you transcends yourself and surpasses your former expectation, you too may know and therefore be more than what you know you are.

You are probably like your peers when you consider the issue of emotion. When students come to college, they tend to limit the range of feelings and emotions they are willing to express. They care deeply what others, particularly of their own age group, think about them. So they do not develop their imagination, but suppress it. The last thing they want is to be different. Striking out on one's own is dangerous. It demands courage. It means to be different. Imagination is for fools. Anguish, failure, self-doubt are to be dulled. Tears and laughter — these are permitted only in careful measure, about some few things.

It is for such as these that Socrates meditates upon the requirements of conscience, that Job speaks of his dead children. For them we tell the story of the Cross and all it stands for; and the suffering and enduring Israel, the Jewish people; the blacks and their historic record of toughness and inner power; and of all the circles of humankind, with their hatreds and resentments, their hopes and unmet aspirations, their fantastic sense of worth, their equally unreal fear of inconsequence. It is closed ears that we want to open, dull eyes we want to brighten, confused minds we want to clarify and expand.

And this we do in the only way open to us: by showing what humanity has been and has made and has thought. This is how people have become more than what they are, and what you, the future and the hope, can feel and do and be and think. Some men and women have known how passionately to care and dream. And we teach the creations of their caring and their passion. It is this you must remember as you choose how you will shape your mind in college.

Chapter Seven

What No Revolution Can Accomplish

We Are What We Are

HE IDEAL WE SOUGHT IN THE 1960s AND the 1970s expressed a dream of education through discovery, growth toward maturity through individual initiative, and learning through students' taking responsibility. But the reality of the revolution proved to be different. While many of us dreamed of intellectual encounter, some professors translated the quest for a new relationship into the search to be liked. Some felt that the good teacher would be the one students liked, the great teacher would be known by jokes, "being with it." These teachers were around before the revolution and were among the many who scarcely grasped its issues. Indeed, the revolution presented an opportunity in its turmoil not to radically revise the processes of higher education but to conveniently exploit them for personal ends, such as a comfortable career. Thus, there were two revolutions, the one in education and another one larger and better documented. This larger and more popular revolution aimed at loosing bonds of discipline and making education appear easier and so more equal.

I know of no campus in which the other revolution — the one now rightly under attack for its degradation of higher education, its loosening of discipline and rejection of rigor — did not demoralize the best and the brightest. For if student response to teaching became a critical issue in tenure decisions (and I believe it should), then who would not want to have popularity among students (and that not necessarily through good teaching at all)? So those of us who had framed a radical theory of education, profoundly conservative in its values, observed a curious development. In the name of our beliefs in scholarship and education, some people, allied in overthrowing snobbery and privilege, placed in their stead a new formalism. If students like me, I must be a good teacher, and that without regard to what and how I teach. If grades preserve "elitism," then no evaluation matters. No student can fail — on principle. Open admission for all who qualify was taken to mean no one needs qualifications. Everyone's opinion is as good as everyone else's, so — people concluded — no one needs to reason with the other. Everything is settled with smiles. Above all, the easygoing, the smiling, the pleasant, the undemanding professor, was the one to celebrate — especially on the part of those who knew precisely what they wanted.

On my own campus in spring 1981, a low-keyed debate was underway on how many courses should be required for a degree. Our so-called new curriculum, then more than a decade old and scarcely examined since its adoption, attracted a renewed measure of interest. To join the discussion, I made up an imaginary speech, one that no one would ever give. It was to be an imagined commencement speech — a fantasy — and you may have heard of it. I was left feeling that nearly everybody in the world listened. I printed it in the student paper. Five thousand undergraduates in my university read it as a personal letter from me to them, individually, and several hundred replied in angry letters. I don't blame them. My message was that the "nice guy" professors, of whom there are too many, cynically avoid responsibilities of conscience and commitment. They ask too little, so they teach all the wrong lessons. Those students who want to be caressed but not taught share the blame for their own undemanding education. They are accomplices in the work of cheating themselves of the reward of achievement through hard work, trial, and learning from error. My target was professors. My arrow hit students.

That message seemed to me self-evident. To me it was so obvious, so good-hearted, that when I printed it in the student paper, I made a bet with a close friend that the paper would receive not a single response. I thought what I said was commonplace, but amusing. It was neither. The paper got something on the order of 200 letters in the next five days, 199 of them declaring me "insane and incompetent," "to be fired from Brown" (at least), and "locked up in an asylum for the criminally insane." Those were the nice letters. I got many more. As I said, the world took note. The paradox caught people's imagination: Students lynch mean professor. Professor tells graduating students they have not learned much. Students tell professor he's a fraud. It was not one of my everyday exchanges.

You can judge this for yourself. This was my imaginary speech, the one no one would ever hear:

"We the faculty take no pride in our educational achievements with you. We have prepared you for a world that does not exist, indeed, that cannot exist. You have spent four years supposing that failure leaves no record. You have learned at Brown that when your work goes poorly, the painless solution is to drop out. But starting now, in the work to which you go, failure marks you. Confronting difficulty by quitting leaves you changed. Outside Brown, quitters are no heroes.

"With us you could argue about why your errors were not errors, why mediocre work really was excellent, why you could take pride in routine and slipshod presentation. Most of you, after all, can look back on honor grades for most of what you have done. So here grades can have meant little in distinguishing the excellent from the ordinary. But tomorrow, in the world to which you go, you had best not defend errors but learn from them. You will be ill-advised to demand praise for what does not deserve it, and to abuse those who do not give it.

"For four years we created an altogether forgiving world, in which whatever slight effort you gave was all that was demanded. When you did not keep appointments, we made new ones. When you were late to class, we ignored it. When your work came in beyond the deadline, we pretended not to care.

"Worse still, when you were boring, we acted as if you were saying something important. When you were garrulous and talked to hear yourself talk, we listened as if it mattered. When you tossed on our desks writing upon which you had not labored, we read it and even responded, as though you earned a response. When you were dull, we pretended you were smart. When you were predictable, unimaginative, and routine, we listened as if to new and wonderful things. When you demanded free lunch, we served it. And all this why? Despite your fantasies, it was not to be bothered, and the easy way out was pretense: smiles and easy B's.

"It is conventional to quote in addresses such as these. Let me quote someone you've never heard of, Professor Carter A. Daniel, Rutgers University, in the *Chronicle of Higher Education*:

> College has spoiled you by reading papers that don't deserve to be read, listening to comments that don't deserve a hearing, paying attention even to the lazy, ill-informed, and rude. We had to do it, for the sake of education. But nobody will ever do it again. College has deprived you of adequate preparation for the next fifty years. It has failed you by being easy, free, forgiving, attentive, comfortable, interesting, challenging, fun. Good luck tomorrow.

"That is why, on this commencement day, we have nothing in which to take much pride.

"Oh yes, there is one more thing. Try not to act toward your coworkers and bosses as you have acted toward us. I mean, when they do not give you what you want but have not earned, don't abuse them, insult them, act out with them your parlous relationships with your parents. This, too, we have tolerated. It was, as I said, not to be liked. Few professors actually care whether or not they are liked by peer-paralyzed adolescents, fools so shallow as to imagine professors care not about education but about popularity. It was, again, to be rid of you. So go, unlearn the lies we taught you. To life!"

Well, that is what I said. How would I say it today? First of all, much less personally. I erred in framing matters as I did, from "me" to "you." It was too broad and encompassing, it was too harsh, it was self-righteous. And it really wasn't me. How do I know? Because the wrong people agreed with me. I got a lot of mail from reactionaries, people habitually angry at the younger generation. But I like students.

As I look back, I understand that I was creating a kind of "persona," the way a playwright does, or a novelist. What would I say if I were . . . ? What would life be like if . . . ? How would I address a graduating class in a memorable way? Now that "I" was not this writer in particular. It was an imaginary "I —" an "I" out there. But quite fairly and correctly, people ignored the headline I gave the little essay, "A Commencement Address You'll Never Hear." (I might have added, " . . . and One I'll Never Give.") They saw my name, and then the message: Boom! Zounds! Pow!

True, the message contained a measure of truth. But not for everyone, not about everyone. It was true, but it was not fair. I paid a heavy price, but I think I helped frame future debates in higher education too. In all, we cannot relive our lives. We can only learn from our mistakes and try not to repeat them.

But it was no mistake to tell the students that we professors really settle for too little and demand not enough. And it was a public service to remind students that the best professors also demand the most and exact the highest achievement of which students are capable. Like everyone else, I make my mistakes in teaching. And you will make your mistakes in learning. But if I have to choose between asking of a student too little or too much, let me err by always asking too much. At least it shows belief and hope. That is what I meant by the ending, "To Life!" That is the goal and purpose of college education: to bring students to life.

Part Two

The Here and the Now

Chapter Eight

Who Should
Go to College?

HE URGENT QUESTION CONCERNS, NOT who in general, but you in particular. Should you go to college? Should you stay there? The answers to these questions are dictated by three factors: motivation, ability, and timing. In addition, we have to consider who should not go to college, and who should not stay there. Let me offer a few simple propositions.

College is not like high school.

College is not higher than high school. It is different. The important difference between high school and college education is the degree of responsibility. The high school teacher takes responsibility for students' learning. The college professor does not. In high school students are carefully watched, monitored through daily quizzes and weekly exams. By contrast, the college course usually involves an hour test in the middle of the semester and a final examination at the end. Further, the college course always requires the student to take full responsibility. No one asks whether the student has done the reading. No one carefully investigates whether or not the student has understood the lectures. This may sound cold and cruel, but it also is the only way for colleges to do their work.

For what the college does is take a half-formed adolescent and send forth an independent citizen. Students come as dependents and leave as independent adults, ready to shape their own lives and define their own careers. What better way to trigger the process of growth to independence than by holding students fully responsible for their own fate? And how better to do it than in the classroom?

In college, in the classroom, mistakes do not have to mark the student as a failure. If a student is irresponsible, the result is a poor grade. If a doctor is irresponsible, the patient may die. If a lawyer is irresponsible, the client may go to jail. If a worker is irresponsible, the company loses and everyone is the poorer. In college mistakes are not permanent; the consequences are limited. After college things change. Knowing this, colleges provide a trial run in the realities of everyday life by making students responsible for themselves and their work. Colleges do not continue the education of high schools; rather they begin the experience of adulthood.

You should go to college if there is something you want to learn there.

Who should go to college? Anyone, at any age, who is ready for college; this means someone who wants to learn what you learn in college. Who should not go to college? Everybody else.

How do you know whether or not you (or your son or daughter) should go to college?

The first consideration is simply your purpose in going. Do you know why you want to go to college? Do you have a clear notion of at least some of the subjects you want to study there? Is college a way of helping you become a particular kind of person? College is not the only option after high school. True, college may look easier than a nine-to-five job, and people assume they will have a better future if they attend college. But most colleges do not offer vocational training. Consequently, if you think the main reason for attending college is to qualify for better jobs, you are wrong. You will end up in college a bored and frustrated person, and you may well quit. Without strong motivation, you will not succeed.

In college students learn a very particular set of subjects. They study literature, history, language, philosophy, mathematics, biology and physics and geology, engineering, education, nursing. There are no courses in patience, courage, loyalty, goodness. There is no specialty in sweeping the streets or washing windows. Among the many things we might teach, we choose only a few. These we teach in one way and not in some other way. We teach through talking about, rather than acting out, through reading and writing. We talk *about* things much more than we do them. In the study of religion, for example, students may analyze the ideas of a prayer book, but they do not pray in class. They may study the purpose, meaning, conduct, and symbolism of sacrifice. But, they do not kill a sheep and burn up its kidneys. In politics students may participate in an election campaign, but mainly as a laboratory exercise. For doers college may present a trial of patience and restraint. We think about things and ask questions more than we try things out. All of this points toward the simple fact that learning takes place in many ways, but college education in only a few.

You must have sufficient reason to study the particular subjects taught in college. Those who really are not interested are not going to learn much, even though they may pass courses. The saddest students, and there are many, really do not know what they are doing in college, even while they earn their degrees.

You should go to college if you have the ability to do the work.

Most colleges and universities today admit nearly everyone who applies; only a small minority pick and choose. Accordingly, you, not the college admissions officer, must decide whether you can succeed in college, and if so, in what kind of study and what sort of college or university.

About half of all Americans of college age find their way to some kind of school of higher education. But if you end up sitting in a classroom and watching others make sense of what to you is gibberish, if you find yourself bored while others are interested, the fault may not lie in the subject or the teacher. (My admittedly self-serving guess is that if you are sufficiently interested in college to read this book, you probably belong there.)

How can you decide whether you should go to college? If you can listen carefully to what another person says and reply to the point that the other has made, you can listen to a lecture and concentrate on it. If you can write to the point and in a cogent way, from beginning to end, you belong in an examination room. If you can express your ideas carefully and accurately, then you will succeed in whatever you do. If you have the patience to follow an argument or an experiment through three or more successive stages, you will do well in the pursuit of learning. If you can read thoughtfully and remember what you have read, you will succeed. These constitute not gifts of heavenly grace but intellectual skills. They are found not only in the gifted but also in people who have been well taught to use the gifts they have. Listening carefully, thinking to the point, responding thoughtfully — these acts of intellect take place in kindergarten as well as in the senior year of high school. Parents who listen to what their children say teach them how to listen, who read to their children teach them how to read, who ask pointed questions of their children teach them how to reason. Parents do the probing, and children do the learning.

You should go to college when you think it is the right time for you.

Tradition brings you to college after high school, usually not before, usually not later. That is the standard pattern. But in college the best students, those with the highest motivation, not uncommonly, have spent a year or two working between high school and college. Or they go into the military. Or they travel. What they accomplish is maturity; they season themselves and develop a range of interests and questions. When they finally turn to college, they understand and appreciate the opportunities. They also have clear goals for themselves. My happiest encounters in the classroom take place with young adults, in their twenties or even in their thirties. They listen with intense interest to what others take to be commonplace truths. The reason is that they have reached that point in life at which higher education answers important questions for them.

If therefore, I could give one fixed rule to every high school student contemplating college, and every college student wondering what he or she is doing there right now, it would be this: Consider the alternatives and try some of them. If you are not sure you belong in college just now, defy the fates and go to work for a year or two. If you are in college and cannot say with clarity and purpose what you are doing there, take a leave of absence. Work or travel, if you can afford it, or consider other forms of advanced education, for example, technical school or an apprenticeship. College is not for everyone, and it surely is not for everyone at the age of eighteen or twenty. If I could persuade people of this proposition, I should contribute materially to human happiness. For if the saddest sort of student is the one who has no reason to study, only slightly less sad are people who, in their twenties, realize what they missed before, when they wasted their college years. It is a waste, it is a tragedy, it is an invitation to needless failure, to send young people to an experience they cannot yet grasp. But we all do it to our children.

As parents we set goals for our children higher than those we have met ourselves, perhaps (if we are wise) other and different ones from ours, but always higher. That is natural for parents, the human condition of failure and disappointment writ small. There is always the mountain we did not conquer. So we want our children to. If you did not go to college, you naturally suppose that something better for your children requires them to go. If you did go to college, you take for granted your children will. They must. And when other people do things, you assume that the time has come for you to do the same. So we all agree that college follows high school as naturally as high tide follows low.

Yet the main cause of failure in college — whether a student gets a degree or not — lies in bad timing. Everyone can learn. Everyone wants to learn. But not everyone can or wants to learn the specific subjects we teach at the very moment in life traditionally scheduled for them. Why do college bells toll — "Come, learn! Ask questions" — at the age of seventeen or eighteen, but rarely at twenty-eight or twenty-nine? It is not because of the natural rhythm of a person's movement toward maturity. It is because of the need for everyone to do pretty much the same thing at the same time for the convenience of the larger society. College tradition does not consider that people do not mature at the same time. They do not enter at the same moment into that realm of questioning that opens its doors to some through speculation and reflection, but to most through tough experience.

Let me be more specific here and suggest what a student might learn from working or traveling. Among the most interested students are those who have worked for a year or two in a foreign country, for they have learned to ask themselves precisely those questions that, in theoretical form, academic learning often raises: how to master a foreign culture, how to explain difference, how to describe, analyze, and interpret another world. We teach best when we can appeal to concrete experience in our students' lives. Students learn best when they can relate what they hear in class to what they know outside. The greater the experience, the greater the learning. Moreover, the learning is not only of an academic nature. Students with experience in a larger world appreciate things that other students do not even notice, for example, a moment of personal concern, a routine courtesy, a casual act of kindness. They know that concern, courtesy, kindness, come as gifts of grace and are not to be taken for granted.

Now that you have read these pages, do you know who should go to college? Young and not-so-young people who want to learn the particular subjects taught there, in the specific ways in which they are taught. And who should not go to college? Those who are not really interested, who cannot explain to themselves why they are in the college classroom and do what they do there. Parents who send unprepared and unmotivated young people to college pay for the professors to serve as the world's most expensive baby sitters.

Chapter Nine

How to Choose a College

HE PROSPECTIVE COLLEGE STUDENT chooses the college. What really counts is whether a college teaches what that student wants to learn. These two perfectly obvious propositions settle a great many questions. What people say about a college, what parents have heard, what the world thinks — none of this should play any role at all. How the prospective student perceives the college and what the student wishes to accomplish there should decide all questions. To help you choose the college that suits you, I will here discuss the individual steps in selecting and evaluating a college.

Deciding How to Decide

Choosing a college is rarely as simple or as reasonable as it should be. Most students choose on the basis of what other people say about the school — its reputation. This can be dangerous for your education and your future. For the paramount trait in the here and the now of higher education in too many places is cant, pretentiousness, boasting — pretending to be more than we are. This is bad for us in universities because we come to believe our own reputations and cease to learn from our mistakes. Rather we should be judged solely by our results unaltered by our clarificatons, justifications, excuses, explanations.

The result is the only criterion that counts. If students judge a college on the basis of the results of the education it offers, the colleges that are now in vogue and considered "the best" may not be judged all that great, and the colleges that people consider unfashionable may turn out to do a very good job for their students over the decades. By a good job, I mean that the alumni emerge able to work with rigor and discipline, to take up the tasks of society: leadership, responsibility, renewal. Think, for instance, of the Catholic colleges such as Providence College, whose alumni govern Rhode Island, and Boston College, whose alumni contribute to the quality of life in Massachusetts. The hewers of wood and drawers of water of higher education, with their Protestant equivalents in the higher educational world of the Middle West and the South, do educate effectively. I lectured at Alverno College, in Milwaukee, to a small group of working people, the first in their families to go on the college, who devote their weekends to higher education and work full time during the week. What could I tell them that they did not know about learning for its own sake and about the rewards of knowing things? They knew the joys of discovery and adventure in ideas and gladly paid for them.

Whether famous or little known, the colleges and universities sustain a system, a pecking order, ratifying self-celebration in universities. Certainly the upper sprig of the Ivy League — Harvard, Yale, Princeton — and its corresponding member, Stanford ("the Harvard of the West Coast"), typify the prejudices people hold about so-called good and bad in colleges.

If there is no good or bad, is there a right and a wrong college for a student? There is no "right" college. But there are many wrong ones for any prospective student. I was no better off than anyone else when I had to help my son search for "the right college" for him. What I discovered even at the outset of the search is that I had little more to go on than any other parent; I was confused and hopeful, and ignorant.

There is a considerable amount of work to be done in identifying possible colleges. Universities that claim distinction — such as the football clubs known collectively as the Ivy League — do not in fact differ significantly from universities that claim, or enjoy, much less distinction. Everyone is the best at something. And there is not all that much difference between one school and the next, especially not in what really happens to students. As a professor who entered the role of parent of a prospective college student, it is the single lesson that most surprised me.

If the distinction of a school is not important, what is? How shall I discover relevant facts, as distinguished from people's self-praise? And how may I escape the poisoned fog of hype that envelops the colleges and universities of this country? Is there a book I should read? Is there a consultant I should approach? Yes, there are good books that purvey not only impressions and self-praise but also facts. There even are consultants who know important and current facts about diverse colleges, and who, further, can recommend a college with particular traits for a student of a distinctive character and interests.

In some areas it is common practice for high school juniors to visit several colleges together in order to decide what schools to apply to. Now a company even organizes bus tours of the New England campuses, to ease the trip. I am not entirely certain that the preapplication visitation proves so common in other regions. But where I teach and in nearby schools, it is. High school juniors come to decide whether or not they will go to Brown or Harvard or Princeton or Wesleyan or Stanford. They must feel wonderful. But a year later, Brown, Harvard, Princeton, Wesleyan, and Stanford make up their minds. Then, in more than a few instances, the high school students feel less wonderful. Reality has made its mark.

What is disheartening about these visits is that students rarely ask the right questions — or, indeed, any questions. In most instances the students are simply not ready for a campus visit and join the tour because it has become the thing to do. The visit to decide whether or not a student will apply to a given school costs hundreds of dollars and saves on the application fee. It would be better to read the relevant catalogs, apply to selected colleges and universities that seem likely, and then wait for results of the competition for admission. *Then visit.* The present order — visit, then application

— is like choosing what you will wear at the Olympics, before you've been chosen for the team.

If you have followed me to this point, you have eliminated gossip and scenery as reasons to apply to a college and you are now ready to do the serious thinking that precedes a choice. Let us consider the basic requirements. If the principal goal in choosing a college is to find a place in which a student can learn, then there are two overriding criteria: (1) the student and (2) the process of learning. What makes possible the process of learning? First, you need books and their equivalent in laboratories. Second, you need teachers. Third, you need a setting in which people can do their work. So there are these three: the means of learning, the men and women of learning, and the setting for learning. The process by which you select possible colleges and then one in particular will revolve around these three elements.

Selecting Colleges

You begin your search with a list of colleges that meet certain requirements, requirements that you define. First and most basic is a subject of study. Does the college offer what you want to study? If it does, this college becomes a possibility and you place it on your list. If the school does not offer what you want, then drop it from any further consideration. You should probably end up with a list of approximately ten to twenty colleges and universities. These schools should meet the following additional criteria.

The second requirement or criterion is location. Is the college located where you wish to spend four years? Some students want to be near home, others do not. The pain of separation for parents and for child becomes anguish when the student travels from one coast to the other, or beyond. But the greater pain of stunted emotional growth for those who live at home when they should go off on their own demands consideration.

You must also ask yourself whether you want to attend college in a country town, such as Hanover, New Hampshire, or a university town, such as Bloomington, Indiana, or Iowa City,

Iowa, or a large city, such as Minneapolis-St. Paul or Boston, or a great metropolis, such as New York City or Los Angeles or Chicago. Each of these types of places has its advantages and disadvantages. A big city offers diversity, cultural opportunities, vivid life. But it may seem threatening. A small town is cozy, pleasant, an extended family. But it may prove stifling. You can make your own list. But don't assume that college life in Chicago is pretty much the same as college life in Champaign-Urbana or Bloomington or Madison.

Third, you can attend a coeducational institution or a single-sex one. There are single-sex colleges, for all men or for all women. I realize that people generally regard a coeducational campus as advantageous. But young people develop at different paces, and relations with the opposite sex prove more threatening for some than for others. More important, in the case of women, the women's college provides the advantage of an unpressured environment, in which young women learn to express themselves vigorously and forthrightly, without suffering on that account. As I shall point out in a different connection, in the classroom men tend to avoid a direct encounter with a woman's ideas. This they do, I have observed, either by ignoring what a woman says or by harassing and hectoring her when she speaks. In a women's college women learn that to be themselves is normal and to express themselves forthrightly is proper and acceptable for women. That argument for women's colleges is not universally accepted. My daughter disagrees with me and so does my wife. But it is something to be considered when choosing a college.

Fourth, you need teachers wherever you go. People outside the university imagine that professors really do live by the adage publish or perish, with the result that the publishing scholars who cannot teach fill the permanent positions, and the perishing scholars who cannot write but can teach drift into advertising or life insurance. Like most generalizations, there is only a little truth in it.

Publishing scholars sometimes teach quite well. A fair number of professors who have nothing to say in print also have nothing to say in class. The real dividing line is between scholars and nonscholars, that is, people who discover things for themselves (whether they say so in print or in class) and people who report what they have learned from others. Some scholars publish, some do not; some nonscholars report vividly and in an exciting way information that in fact was obtained at third or fourth hand. Others repeat in a boring way things they have heard and grasped only in a dull spirit. How can you tell the difference in advance? I can propose negative indicators: most people who have not published a book by forty will not publish one afterward. But they may keep up and have much to teach. More relevant to you is the number of professors in the program you want to study in. Is there a department with Ph.D.'s? Are there only M.A.'s? How many professors teach how many courses? How many areas does one professor teach? Does one professor carry six courses, all at an introductory level? These are questions you can answer by carefully reading the catolog. A small department will be limited in what it can offer to students, a larger department will have greater variety.

A fifth requirement is the religious environment. If you are a religious person or derive from an ethnic group with distinctive interests, do not imagine that in college you can live your religious life just as you did beforehand. Make sure that the institutions and requirements of your religion thrive on campus. Catholics, for instance, should make sure that the necessities of a religious way of life are available. Be certain that people of your religious tradition find themselves respected. Jews should consider very carefully whether they will enjoy life as the only Jew on campus.

Students leave high school in the fantasy that, in college, everyone is pretty much the same. You can stop being "different," because you leave the home and family that mark you as different. But college is not the beginning of life; it is only a new phase. You leave a Jewish home, or a Catholic home, or an evangelical home, and you take with you emotions and convictions, beliefs about God and about what is good and bad that your family and home nurtured in you. If you think that, in college, you stop being Jewish, Catholic, black, or a vitally active woman, and begin a life in which pretty much everyone is the same as everyone else and everybody loves everybody, you have some jarring discoveries in prospect.

In all, Catholics should avoid colleges in which professors all know as fact that there is no God. Blacks should avoid colleges in which they are only tolerated. Jews should avoid colleges in which they are thought odd and especially interesting. People of Hispanic heritage should avoid colleges in which they find no provision for their cultural and ethnic expression. Universities today make more provision for diversity. Make sure you fit in.

A sixth requirement is one that few of you may have considered yet and this is athletics. The four years of college divide the good athletes from the others. The able ones go out for teams. For them colleges provide coaches and facilities. Athletes enjoy endless attention, even adulation, as they grow and mature. They are well cared for. I am worried about the nonathletes. No one cares whether after high school they continue to exercise, enjoy sports, participate. But everyone, at all ages, must use the body as much as the mind. Not only health, but also mental well-being demand that we keep ourselves active. Those who are physically lazy ridicule the others, to be sure, but they are the ridiculous ones. How a college or university treats the less important athlete can be an important measure of the attention given to the individual at that school.

When you consider colleges, if you are not a great athlete, find out whether there are ample chances for you to play the sports you enjoy. Ask, also, whether other students spend at least a few hours a week — five at a minimum — in athletics, or whether the atmosphere keeps people sedentary and ''intellectual.'' In addition to the other endless possibilities of the college years, you should want to try sports you have never played. Does the college provide the chance to learn, even including coaches for nonathletes? Can you do things you have never done before, and get help? If you can, then that college understands its job. Don't be impressed by the stadium that seats seventy-five thousand people. Look for the dozens of playing fields for the hundreds and thousands of student athletes who will never play in the stadium.

By the time you have compiled a list of colleges and universities that meet the six criteria listed you will have learned much about the differences between and similarities among schools. You are now ready to narrow the field to a few schools that seem best suited to your goals.

Narrowing the Field

You and your parents should now consider the specific academic program and the degree of freedom of choice in the colleges and universities on your list. You as a student should be able to pursue your distinctive interests and build on their strengths. Consider the following points when you are ready to narrow your list.

> (1) A better college may have fewer fixed degree requirements rather than more. (2) A better college will have more departments (centers, programs, institutes) offering majors rather than fewer. (3) A better college will allow professors to be autonomous of their departments, rather than treating them as cogs in the wheel of a smoothly running vehicle. (4) A better college will give students a wide range of individual freedom to shape programs along lines of their own interests.

In listing these ways of evaluating an academic program, I mean only to stimulate your imagination. If I can point to details that seem to speak about the whole, then you will pick out other details that escape my attention entirely. When parents and prospective students visit the campus, they should know what is important to them in particular: the kind of program the college or university offers, the way in which courses are conducted, the character of the faculty, the composition of the student body, the living environment of the students, and any other evidence that education goes on as it should. When high school students visit, they commonly notice trivial, often accidental things — the person they happened to meet that day, the speech mannerisms of their student guide. No decision matters more, at that point in life, than the choice of a college or university. Yet, in my observation and experience, none rests on a more flimsy basis. It is as if, on the basis of a single anecdote, you decided whom you will marry.

The Campus Visit

The final element in your decision will be what you learn on a visit to the college or university. I said earlier that you should not plan a visit until after you have been accepted, but I recognize that most students and their parents will want to see the school before they apply, so I here offer a guide to the campus visit.

The Student Body

While students come and go, the characteristics of a student body persist. If you doubt that, compare the students at West Point with those at the University of California at Berkeley, or, if you like, take the subway from Harvard to MIT, or fly from Brigham Young University in Provo to SUNY at Stony Brook. The obvious distinctions — clothing, manner of speech — mean little by themselves, but they may well signify deeper differences. Neat clothing and short haircuts, such as you find at Brigham Young, need not stand for orderly thinking. But they do suggest that the students follow one set of rules rather than another. I suspect that the scruffy and unkempt students of larger urban universities work as hard at appearing messy as the BYU students work at looking like straight arrows. The point is that the distinctions in clothing, speech, carriage, may signal deeper differences. A student who is carefully groomed will do well to note the dress of the students in colleges under examination, so too the opposite.

Women and Minorities

If you are a woman or a member of a minority, you will want to consider the student body from another angle. Is there room for you? Will you be made welcome? Will you feel comfortable? I have already dealt with these issues above when I discussed religious considerations. The school you choose should want you for what you are — not to fill a quota or round out a program. If your peers are comfortable, you probably will be too.

If you are not a woman or a minority, there is still one point to consider. Will you be comfortable going to a school that does not recognize the worth of the large numbers of different kinds of people in this country? Will you be happy with cultural or ethnic isolation? Does your program require you to attend a school with a limited population? Can you compensate for this?

The Library and Other Resource Centers

A university with a substantial collection of books in open stacks so that students can browse offers readers an endless adventure. When they hear about a book, they can go and find it, look into it, consider reading it. A university with a mediocre collection offers students frustration and disappointment. And if the library has closed stacks, students miss the joys of browsing; they hear about books but cannot see them. Undergraduates do not need million-volume collections; they *can* make do with two or three hundred thousand volumes. But schools vary widely in the size of their libraries, and the serious student should consider this. The same consideration obviously applies to laboratories, computer facilities, and the like.

You should also note the hours of libraries and computer centers. It costs money to keep these facilities open. Poor colleges curtail library hours, rich ones may keep libraries open deep into the night. It matters if you plan to study long hours — or your own, odd hours. In my view an ideal college will keep the computer center, library, and all laboratories open twenty-four hours a day.

Intellectual Life

Library hours are also a measure of the intellectual life of the school. If the libraries are open for long hours, and are used on Saturday nights or at other unlikely times, then students are serious about their work. When I came to Brown, the first thing I noticed was that the library tended to be as busy on a Saturday evening as on a Thursday afternoon.

Also look at the bookstores near the campus. Do they sell only textbooks and souvenirs? Or do you find a wide selection of books anyone might purchase, even when not required to? Do you see magazines that cover the world of learning, or do you see the same mass market selection available at an airport?

Look at the student publications. If the student paper covers the campus seriously and raises issues thoughtfully, the students may form a mature and responsible community. If the paper is shrill or strident or just plain silly and trivial, the editors and reporters may stand for little more than their own immaturity. Are there many papers and magazines? Or just a few?

Find out whether lectures outside of courses attract good numbers of students, and, if so, which lectures in particular. If students live a life of curiosity and search, then they will come to hear visiting lecturers and learn about different viewpoints, diverse perspectives. A campus in which students neglect the extracurriculum — the program of lectures, concerts, plays, art exhibits, and other modes of intellectual expression — attracts bored and boring young people. When you visit, see what is going on. Ask students when they last listened to someone who was not a teacher in a classroom. The answers, including the evasions, will prove illuminating.

The Faculty

You cannot expect to evaluate the faculty, but you should be aware of their standing. When considering the faculty, ask to see the publication record. Take it seriously, and do not (as most do) dismiss the publishing scholar as a poor teacher. If the question interests you, take the trouble of looking up the book of a professor and perhaps even opening it. In other words, exercise your own taste and judgment.

The Classroom

Visiting a classroom will give you crucial information. Do the students simply write things down? Or can you detect a process of intellectual engagement? Does the professor aim at entertaining the students, holding their attention with jokes? Or does the professor get wrapped up in the excitement of the subject? Students' powers to listen intently may be tested by the dull professor, but listen to what the dull one *says*. You may discover a person at the frontier of learning, leading students across the frontier into an unknown. That is not dull, even if the setting — a monotonous voice, a talking head — may contradict the vivid content.

Look at the students in the class as they ask and answer questions. Do they all look comfortable? Are the comments made by women listened to and responded to respectfully? Or are the women belittled, patronized? Do the students of all groups find the material interesting?

As you attend classes, ask yourself whether you would like to do what the students around you are doing. Go to classes that are part of required courses, go to seminars if you can, go to upper level classes, visit laboratories, ask questions in the library and find out whether the staff is helpful or indifferent.

A Final Choice

You have made a short list, applied to schools, and made a few visits; perhaps you have even postponed the campus visit until after you have been accepted. You wait as patiently as you can. The letter arrives. You are rejected.

What happens if you choose the college, but the college does not choose you? Let me close with a word of comfort to any of you young readers who do not get into the college of your choice. Or you find yourself in a more difficult predicament — you are on a waiting list. You may not hear from the first-choice school until late August. Let me say with deep feeling: *No school is worth your anguish.* None is so much better than another that you should regard yourself as rejected, your life as blighted, if you have to go to college A rather than to college B.

Let me tell you the story of a wise admissions officer. At first he admitted students who clearly regarded his college as their safety school or their second choice. Why? Because they were the "best" students he could find. By all the averages they looked desirable. But many of them chose to go elsewhere. Those who came presented a problem. They regarded his college — which now was theirs — as second best. They regarded themselves as rejects. Their college was as much a failure as they were. So what did he decide to do? He began to admit prospective students who found in his college exactly the things they wanted — small, pleasant, in a lovely neighborhood and a charming old town, with a faculty that cared for the students, and an administration that believed in the college's future. Now the students who came to that college — maybe not statistically so impressive as before — rejoiced in that college. They were precisely where they wanted to be. They declared their college to be the Garden of Eden, their lives to be pure joy. They went and told the world that theirs was the greatest college in the world. They were proud to be there and proud of themselves. Nothing had changed except for one thing: the students' attitude toward themselves. But that changed the face of the college, and nothing has ever been the same. That college was Brown University, and that change took place in the late 1960s and early 1970s. We became the most popular university in America at just that time.

Everything depends upon your own self-respect. You cannot place in the hands of an admissions officer something so valuable as your heart. You are what you are, and you are not greater if you get into your first-choice school or less if you do not. You will make the best of life's opportunities and your own gifts — if you believe in yourself. If you do not have confidence in yourself and respect yourself, then you will be defeated by disappointment.

In concrete terms, again with emphasis: *Do not accept a place on anybody's waiting list.* Go to the school that both accepts you and most closely resembles the sort of school you want. Do not be taken in by people's boasting about their college and then suffer disappointment if you are not admitted. Withhold judgment until you are admitted, and then take seriously the schools that want you. I have spent my entire career in Ivy League universities. Believe me, they have no monopoly on great scholarship — far from it. They have no corner on good teaching or happy student life. They offer a good education. So do a great many other colleges and universities. That is a simple fact. Please accept it from me. If you are not admitted to the school you really thought you wanted, but you are admitted to one lower down on your list, go to that school with respect for the school and regard for yourself.

Greatness comes from within. Achievement is what you do, not what other people say. Lives of worth and service take shape in every kind of circumstance. We are what we do, and not what people say about us. If you are disappointed, pick up your life and go on. You are better for it. So too will be the many people to whose disappointment you can relate because of your own, the many whose lives will be better and richer because of you.

Chapter Ten

Courses and Careers

E IN UNIVERSITIES HAVE A SINGLE PUR-
pose: to open minds to new ideas. Yet peo-
ple who send us their children and the young
men and women who come to us often expect us to do something quite different. Education is pushed into the background, and
the purpose of college may be lost. Let me list some of the
things people expect from universities.

First, we serve as a means of determining who will undertake what kind of work: who will be doctors and lawyers and
who will work in factories. As more and more areas of work
require degrees, more and more people find their futures determined by a college admissions officer. Should that kind of
selection process be made the responsibility of the schools?
We do not know for sure, but my feeling is no. Lawyers once
learned their craft by a strict apprenticeship rather than a
course of study; successful businessmen need to know things
schools cannot teach — how to gamble, how to evaluate people on the spot. There is no reason why these skills should
be learned after college.

Second, we serve as a means of bringing about social change.
We are expected to change students, in part through what we
teach. Whether students are expected to change their man-
ners or their morals, schools are entrusted with the task and
the responsibility to serve as guardians, critics, models. What
the home cannot do with three fourths of the day, the public
schools are supposed to do in the other fourth. What the first

eighteen years have not witnessed, the four years of college are supposed to bring about.

We teach math. Society expects us to produce conscience. We teach the correct usage of the English language. Society demands that we educate tomorrow's leaders, tomorrow's workers. Above all, we teach skills of mind meant to serve a lifetime. Students want us to give them skills to sell in the marketplace tomorrow. We teach habits of work and habits of thought. People expect us to find them jobs.

The expectations laid at our feet bear little relationship to what we know how to do. We are asked to signify who is smart and who is not; to serve as instruments of social change; to bring about moral regeneration; and to impart the salable skills of the moment. This is not the purpose of a college education.

A liberal education teaches students how to work, but it does not give them skills in a particular job. It teaches the disciplines of logical thinking, clear and accurate expression, sustained analysis, but it does not give an easy formula for solving a specific problem. Whether students study chemistry, geology, sociology, or philosophy, whether they master a foreign language or mathematics, or history or religious studies, they learn nothing they can sell to an employer tomorrow, but they gain a great many things they can draw upon through a long career of useful work.

Whenever there is a change in the economy, students become conscious of the financial realities of life, but this awareness cannot change what goes on in a college. We professors shall not teach you students how to type or how to repair or program a computer. These are salable skills today, but they may well be obsolete tomorrow. There are other places prepared to teach these things. We shall teach you how to compose your thoughts into a paragraph someone else will want to read, how to express yourself in a language other than our own, how to analyze properties of the natural world and qualities of society, how to frame and answer questions. These intellectual powers will always be with you. Whatever technical skill you gain for a specific career will be hollow without the depth of your mind. A logical mind, strengthened through philosophy courses or mathematics, will approach the technical skill of the computer programmer with far less doubt and far greater confidence than the mind of one who has only sought marketable skills.

Students do not invent on their own this quest for a marketable skill. In many instances, the parents present obstacles to their childrens' choice of study. They want to know what the student can do with the major. They mean, can the student make a living with it? And parents do not like the answer to their question. Most of the fields of the liberal arts cannot supply knowledge that is immediately salable. True, chemistry or applied math or engineering majors can get jobs in their fields of concentration, while classicists, historians, and students of religions cannot. That is true, but it is trivial compared to what all students attain if they choose the right major for themselves. The real issue is learning how to think and growing toward maturity. The tangential question of what the student will do afterward answers itself in due course. Rarely does the answer derive from what has been learned in the classroom, but it always depends upon what has happened on the campus. Parents who themselves went to college should ask how much on an everyday basis they use what they learned many years ago, and to what extent their earning capacity rests upon what they chose as a major. Then they will allow their sons and daughters the freedom to choose.

In the exercise of your powers to learn to criticize an idea or a picture, how to take apart and put together an event of history or a piece of literature, you learn that there are things worth knowing and saying beyond the weak "Well, that's my opinion." The difference between an educated person and an uneducated one is that the educated person is not reduced to saying merely, "Well, that's my opinion," but can also say why that is his or her opinion. Further, people of learning can attempt to persuade another person that an opinion is sound and should be adopted. And in this the educated person demonstrates an important lesson of his or her education. This is a lesson you shall learn, and it opens many doors. This is that discourse between intelligent people has rules, rules that acknowledge the mutual respect of scholars as people. You will listen, respond, question, disagree, probe, consider. You will never become angry or belittling. If you abandon respect for your partner in dialogue, you abandon your position as an educated person.

Liberal education aims at giving you the power to use your mind. It is meant to give you the experience of thought, of critical learning and careful expression of your ideas, of listening to others and responding to the point. Now, I recognize these skills are not highly prized — until they are missing from common discourse. When people discover they cannot grasp what others are saying or they cannot make comprehensible what they want to say, they realize what they have not learned in college. When in business or the professions you find out that mere technology does not suffice to do the work, that you have to think through problems freely and solve dilemmas imaginatively, you find out what intellectual powers you have, and have learned to use, in a liberal education.

Yet even if these things we teach were of little social value, instead of serving, as they do, as the bridge from mind to mind, they would still count. For we are not made out of flesh and bones alone. We are by our nature thinking people, reflective and questioning. The substance of life is not merely to eat and sleep. It also is to attain consciousness about ourselves and our lives. All of us sometimes are philosophers, in the old sense of the word: We are people who love to know things, who love wisdom. By our nature we question, learn, respond to the world we perceive — not merely experience. That is why a liberal education is essential. It is not merely for making a living, but for living a worthwhile life.

Let us turn from the ends to the means. Exactly how should you choose your courses — when you have a choice? There are four reasons for choosing a course.

You should choose what is new, a challenge, something your mind has not encountered before. Entering students naturally assume that at college they will do things they already have done, but at a higher level. That is why freshmen commonly select subjects they have studied in high school: history, English, a foreign language, chemistry, math. It takes a year to persuade freshmen to take subjects they have never studied, such as art, classics, music, economics, or psychology, or did not even know existed, such as philosophy, black history, Judaic or women's studies, sociology, urban studies, Afro-American studies, and semiotics. There is nothing wrong with history, English, math, a foreign language. But one thing you should do right from the start is explore new areas.

If students come to college expecting to study the same subjects as in high school, they come expecting very different relationships with their teachers. Students expect to know, and be known by, their professors, Yet if you take four courses, each with more than fifty students, you probably will never know a professor as a person. If you are typical of most students, you may take two or even three years to reach those courses of modest size in which professors know you, and you know them. If you want professors to know you, you must find at the outset at least one course in which a senior professor can identify you as a student and as a person. Professors cannot reach out to you if you are one of two hundred students he or she teaches each semester. You are the one who must make the effort.

You may also select a course in order to study with the professor who gives it — whatever that teacher teaches, and however large or small the class. Although education is learning facts, it is also learning how first-rate minds work. Ideally, the subjects you want and need to study will be taught by first-class intellects who show how they work while they work. As they work they provide a model of mind. But often what you need to study and the person with whom you ought to study do not coincide. You should select at least a few courses that will enable you to study with truly distinguished scholars, especially those who want to teach as well as contribute to learning. Every year read the list of faculty members and take courses by those who are respected scholars or highly regarded teachers.

Finally, some courses impart information and other courses undertake sustained inquiry, analysis of problems, testing of possibilities. Try to take those courses that exercise your mind, in preference to courses that merely teach you things you want to know. The courses that demand analytical effort may tax your abilities and test your confidence — math and philosophy, for instance. You may have to listen more carefully, think more slowly, and speak more thoughtfully than you are used to doing. That is all to the good. Try to take at least one course a semester in which you acquire not only information but also powers of analysis.

More specifically, you should select courses that will teach you to write. In the social sciences and humanities, take a course in which you present papers for close criticism. The most important step you take is learning to use your mind to unpack an idea lucidly, on the one side, and accurately express it, on the other. You will come to understand that good writing is not a gift or an accident: It is knowing the right word and using it correctly, and clarifying an idea in all its implications.

If you have clear-cut career goals, you know that these will require you to take one set of courses rather than another. Students in engineering, premedical programs, prelaw courses, and the like often find their choices limited. In the same way students who undertake two concentrations will not be able all the time to obey all the rules I have offered. And that is so, even though they may agree with the reasoning I offer. But if among your courses in a given year there are at least some that meet the criteria I have outlined, then you should enjoy a stimulating and interesting year of study.

If, on the other hand, you sit in large classes and take notes, repeat them on exams, and walk out unknown to your teachers, if you spend your first year learning more about essentially the same subjects you studied in high school, if you miss the more challenging and controversial teachers at college, and if for the most part you just learn facts rather than think through ideas and problems, the fault is yours.

For in choosing courses you bear responsibility for your mistakes — and also for your successes. That is the only way you will grow up. It is growing up in mind and soul and spirit and heart that the university is here to help you to accomplish.

Chapter Eleven

What People Learn in College
The Major

HE MOST PROMINENT FEATURE OF COL-
lege, in most people's minds and in fact, is
the major or the field of concentration. When
you meet a college student, you ask first,
Where do you go to college? Then you ask,
What's your major? What people say about
the major dominates discussion — not what people learn
in it, not how people benefit from it. And since college education costs a lot of money, people want to know how they
can make a living with what they learn — hence, with what
they learn in their major. Who can blame them? But they
really are wrong. In later life your major matters very little,
and after college few will ask you about it. What you study
matters less than what happens to you because of what you
study. And you may grow intellectually and emotionally in
chemistry as much as in applied math, in the study of religion or of music or of history as much as in political science or sociology, let alone business administration, journalism, nursing, and home economics. Every subject may contribute to your growth in mind and heart and spirit, and any
subject may be turned into mind-numbing and soul-killing
technicalities.

Well, just what is a major? Who defines and controls a major? Who sells it? Who benefits by having college education
organized around the major?

First, "major" or "field of concentration" is that area in
which a student takes about a quarter to a third or even half
of the courses required for the degree, and in which the level

of courses generally proceeds from elementary to advanced. The major thus defines the subject or area the student learns with special emphasis. It is the one field, among many, about which students are supposed to be well informed. Accordingly, the challenge of the junior and senior years reflects the rewards of sustained learning, or the major. Here, it is clear, students focus their attention and time; they progress onward and upward, and they move from being passive recipients of facts to being active participants in the quest for learning. They rise to those mature levels of intellect — in some one, specific subject, to be sure — to which, in coming to college, they aspire. What stands behind the idea of a major? First, the theory, then, the politics. And then the strategy for developing a major.

Theory

The theory is that the human sciences organize themselves in one of two ways. They seek general rules, applicable in a broad range of human worlds ("cultures," "societies," and other historical entities). These rules form such disciplines as psychology, history, sociology, anthropology, or the historical study of religion; they come from anywhere and apply everywhere. For these rules, specific human worlds serve as exemplary materials, that is, we see how history or sociology or the science of politics works in one country or another. The other mode of organization — when rightly done it will complement the first — focuses upon the distinctive traits of a particular human world. You study one small subject and seek to interpret that subject in such a way as to make it tell you about the broader human condition. You study, for instance, American history or French literature or the experience of women through history. In those specific subjects, you learn about what it means to be a human being in America, what it means to use your imagination in France, how a particular sex encounters the issues of life common to both.

In theory, universities organize work in the human sciences in both of these ways, with disciplinary departments, such as political science, sociology, and history, in which the same methods apply to a diversity of problems and settings, and with interdisciplinary departments, such as classics, Egyptology, religious studies (involving both history and philosophy of religion), and American, Slavic, black, women's, or Judaic studies. In these departments, people bring a broad range of questions to a particular human world. Both modes of organizing learning prove their worth every day. No student's education is complete without a systematic acquaintance with each. In the one the student learns to see things whole and all together; in the other, the student learns to see things in detail and with respect for difference, specificity, and even the imponderable of what seems private and particular, yet addresses the human condition as everyone knows it. The hard sciences, for their part, focus upon the natural world — its biology, its chemistry, for instance — and through that one thing teach method about how to study everything. So much for the theory. Now to the politics.

Politics

The major reflects the power of the department and the politics of the university. If professors are influential, then the subject they teach will attract attention and financial support; if they are not, then their subject will be labeled trivial or unimportant. Both subjects may prove equally significant, but politics will dictate which set of courses thrives and which one perishes. When, for example, a university faculty decides which subjects form the "core" of the curriculum (that is, the group of courses to be required), these chosen subjects are frequently those taught by the professors in the room the day they voted on a new curriculum. When choosing a college or a major, take this fact into account. If you want to study foreign languages, and the budgets of the departments that teach foreign languages are being cut back, then that is not the college for you. If the major you wish to pursue is taught by a department not held in high esteem, then go to a college in which it is.

Departments usually define majors. Given what we claim a major is, we should expect that the nature and structure of a discipline or subject should define the rules of mastering that subject or discipline. If a major is supposed to present a well-organized and systematic process of learning a given subject, then a major should emerge logically from the definition and structure of that subject, first things first, second things second, unimportant things never. But too often that is not how it works.

The program of courses required by a major is haphazard. Rarely do departments define the purpose of the major; or if they do, rarely do they define it in terms of what students actually do and how courses really lead students from level to level. The well-organized and logically structured majors usually come from the natural sciences and mathematics, engineering and computer science departments, rarely from the social sciences, and never from the humanities. In fields in which knowledge is factual and set, rather than a function of taste and judgment, a major can be constructed as a composition of logical progression from fact to fact, skill to skill, method to method. Try learning calculus without algebra, and you'll see what I mean.

In the humanities and in most of the social sciences, the major often presents a mishmash of what professors happen to be teaching that year. True, many departments will offer what they call a methods course, by which they mean a course in the basic approaches, questions, and problem-solving techniques of the subject. Or, at the very least, they will present a course bearing the lowest possible number, for example, 1, and let people assume that that course introduces the subject. After all, it stands before No. 2, No. 20, or No. 200. But if you look into that introductory course in English, history, religious studies, and the like, you see, for good or ill, nothing either less, or more, elementary than what you see in courses that allegedly rest upon and build upon that introductory course. These second and third level courses will strike you as more specific and limited in focus. They will be, for example, not about Europe in the twentieth century, but about the causes of World War I; not about the formation of the American nation, but about theories of the American revolution.

The description of the subject explains only what is covered. It rarely indicates that the methods or disciplines, the intellectual challenge of the course, stand upon a foundation already laid down. The upper level course may not even take for granted information already mastered in an earlier course. For the truth is that, in general, the humanities and a fair part of the social sciences do not present subjects that allow for system, for the logical unfolding of methods or techniques. When we deal with issues of taste and judgment, experience in reflection and wisdom, what orderly sequence leads step by step from the ignorant to the wise person?

A major is meant to balance the diffuse and diverse curriculum, within which a student makes choices, by setting up a cogent and coherent segment of the curriculum for a student's close attention. But the major may well present diffusion and diversity on a small scale. Rather than redefine the subject and how it is taught, a department will set requirements that will give the appearance of order, structure, and logic, in order to validate its existence as a department, as a coherent field of study. You must keep this in mind when you begin to develop your major.

The great educator, Jonathan Z. Smith, who served as dean of the college at the University of Chicago, phrases the matter succinctly in *Choice*:

> In most cases, departments and majors lack coherence because they are neither subject matters nor disciplines. Rather than the principled stipulation of a domain of inquiry (a perfectly legitimate endeavor), they are the result of a series of gentlemen's agreements. Take, as an example, a department or a major in English literature — frequently one of the larger and most politically self-conscious units on campus. Scholars in English employ a host of methods, not one of which is unique to their field of inquiry, most of which are shared with the majority of other departments in the humanities and, increasingly, with the social sciences as

well. Nor is there any coherent limit, any modesty, to their domain. Almost anything printed
from left to right in Roman type may be
taught: from Greek tragedies to world literature; from myth to mysticism; psychoanalytic
theory, social anthropology, popular literature,
technical texts.

Smith sees the first course in the major as a well-organized
survey. The last course provides for individual research of
some kind. But he says, "What comes in between is political
rather than substance: a course with each of the major professors." He further argues that when people plan degrees,
majors, and courses, they make choices. Since no one can, or
would want to, learn everything about everything, all of education begins in a set of choices. He therefore holds that
whatever we do requires justification and rationalization:

> I take as a corollary to this that each thing
> taught or studied is taught or studied not be-
> cause it is "there," but because it is an exam-
> ple, an *exempli gratia* of something fundamen-
> tal that may serve as a precedent for further
> interpretation and understanding. By providing
> an arsenal of skills and paradigms from which
> to reason, that which may first appear to be
> strange or novel can become intelligible.
>   Given this: that each thing which is taught is
> taught by way of an example and that the cur-
> riculum is an occasion for institutional choice,
> then the primary choice is: What shall the
> things taught exemplify? This ought to be ex-
> plicit in every academic endeavor, at every
> level of the curriculum.

He further concedes explicitly:

> To these matters of choice and exemplifica-
> tion, no single answer can be given. These
> must remain institutional choices which fit

each institution's peculiar ecology. But we may demand that they be articulated, and tested for, and that the goals be explicitly built into every course of study and not left for accidental discovery by a student. Students ought not to be asked to organize and integrate what the faculty will not. Distribution requirements — whether at the level of general education or the middle-range of the major, violate these two injunctions at will.

Once we recognize that the curriculum, the major, the department, come to us because of a combination of political and intellectual circumstances, we face a new set of tasks. We must make up our minds about issues on which "the experts" cannot help us. Departments do not usually exhibit intellectual coherence. It follows that human knowledge — "everything about everything" — will not reach us when considerations other than intellectual ones intervene in how that knowledge finds definition and categorization. If the bulk of what we know as true constitutes the outcome of processes of taste and judgment, as much as weighing and measuring, then the individual's power to exercise that taste, that judgment, should predominate. And this is the premise to follow in defining your major.

Choosing a Major
Exactly how, then, should you choose your major? Precisely the way you choose your courses — but much more carefully. Here are the criteria that seem to me decisive:

1. The major should be offered by a strong department and be made up of courses taught by first-rate professors. Do not choose a major merely because the subject interests you. If the professors who give the courses that make up the major are boring or trivial, they will rapidly persuade you that the subject of the major is not so interesting. The

department should offer lectures by guests
and other extracurricular programs.
2. The major should take up a subject that interests you. Even the greatest professor of
mathematics could not turn me into a math-
ematician, though I loved the subject. At
some point, at about stage three of any the-
orem, I always end up asking myself why I
have to know all this. You too should know
in your heart why you must know the subject at hand, the major you have chosen.
3. The major should concern a subject or discipline that you think you would like to continue to study after college. It should bear so
immediately and in such an important way
upon your long-term plans that you can imagine continuing the study twenty years
after college.
4. The major should not direct you, the month
after college, into a particular job. It should
not provide those skills that will permit you
to make your living right away. If it does,
you may find those skills obsolete, as knowledge grows and technology changes. What is
relevant today to how you make a living may
prove irrelevant to making a living tomorrow.

If you think Number 1 contradicts Number 2 and Number
3 contradicts Number 4, you are not totally wrong. What I am
suggesting is that you balance your decisions so that your education turns out to be both intellectually stimulating and personally interesting, long-lasting, and in some ways useful.

Still, what matters most is the intellectual strength, the scholarly commitment and vitality, the academic authenticity of the
professors in the department you choose. Take as an example
a field I know well: the academic study of religion. The field
attracts students because of the intrinsic interest of the subject of religion, to which most people, in this country,

are exposed as they grow up. When you consider the issues addressed in the study of religion, you cover the whole range of human knowledge and experience: culture, society, literature, art, music, dance, how we feel and how we think, all in relationship to God, history, and eternity. Yet the field of religion as an academic subject has yet to define for itself high standards of learning, even appropriate subject matter and an ongoing curriculum. So people can teach anything they want and call it "religion," because religion is anything people say it is. And anyone can declare himself or herself not just a person who professes a religion but a professor of religion. So here I find Numbers 1 and 2 in serious conflict, since you can study a great subject with frauds and know-nothings.

The conflict of Numbers 3 and 4 is more obvious. Prelaw students used to think they should study Latin, because the law books use Latin phrases. These days that notion seems out of date. But today prelaw students imagine they should study political science or government, just as prebusiness students take for granted they should study economics, and premedical students biology. And the engineers-to-be take a lot of engineering courses. And why not? These students are not wrong, but they often limit themselves too early in life to subjects they will learn better and more currently later on. Worse, they close doors they should leave open. Later on they may feel a sense of inadequacy about such subjects as literature, art, music, history, and philosophy and not read related books or go to plays *they* would enjoy. More important, they may discover that what they think does not matter to lawyers, doctors, engineers, and women and men in business because they are not well rounded enough to speak of critical issues and concerns to people in all those professions. So choose your major with those same considerations of balance and proportion that go into the selection of your courses.

One final thought: In choosing your major, don't forget that after college you're allowed to read books. In the four years of college you don't have to learn everything you're ever going to know. So in choosing your major, you might even leave something for later.

Chapter Twelve

Who Teaches

Professors and Teaching Assistants

HE WORK OF A TEACHER IS TO SPEAK about ideas in an effective manner. A teacher has to keep students alert and attentive. A teacher has to teach students how to listen, before teaching what to hear, and a teacher has to teach the students how to think two or three related, logically connected thoughts, before teaching what problems to solve and how to solve them. A teacher has to know how to listen, what to listen to, to recognize the signs of being heard, to read the signs of being tuned out. For our work is to enter into minds and so to change lives. No one successful in life today, rich in achievement and heavy in responsibility, would have succeeded were it not for teachers who gave us access to our own capacity of mind.

I write as a teacher, because it is all I have ever been or ever wanted to be. In this regard we professors really are different from presidents, provosts, deans. We do not want their jobs. We who live our lives in classrooms and in studies are doing the things we were created to do. We want no more, because we think we have it all. When we list our heroes, moreover, they turn out to be the founders and framers of our civilization. Who are the greatest teachers of all time, if not Socrates, Jesus, and Moses? What did Socrates do, if not walk the streets and argue with everybody, all the time, everywhere, about anything simple and obvious, like what is truth? What did Moses do, if not instruct his people, not always kindly, not always patiently, but always passionately, about what they should be? What teacher can fail to admire and envy the pedagogical power of Jesus, who could capture a world of meaning and present it whole and complete in a parable? While I have listed three male founders of our civilization, all of us may list the women closer at hand who in our own lives and times did no less for each of us than the pedagogue-founders of the West did for us all.

What makes a good teacher, then, is clear. A good teacher is someone who can enter into the mind of another person and bring to life the mind of that other person. A good teacher does the work by arguing, pressing, asking questions, challenging answers, asking more questions. The life of the good teacher is expressed in giving life to ideas, imparting meaning to what appears to lie entirely beyond intellect, making the obvious into a problem, turning the world of settled truths into an adventure. A good teacher is argumentative, disorderly, prepared for confrontation everywhere, all the time, with everyone, on everything — all for the sake of the vital mind, the freely inquiring spirit. And make no mistake about it: If you can reason, someone somewhere has criticized you. If you can think clearly, someone has listened carefully to what you have said and has corrected you — and corrected you in such a way that you heard and grasped the connection. Great teachers are the foundation of our vitality as people, of our capacity as a society to do our work. These teachers are all around us. It should then be no wonder to you that someone would write with pride, "I am a teacher, and it is all I ever wanted to be, and all I ever want to be."

In liberal arts colleges and some universities, all the classroom teaching is done by professors, people who hold doctorate degrees in the fields in which they teach. But in all large universities, private and public, much teaching is done by graduate students, people en route to their doctorate degrees, who are advanced students in the field they now profess. So formal education — as distinct from the real work of learning — occurs in the classroom at the hand of two sorts of teachers, those who have completed their formal education, and those who have nearly done so.

Professors

In Chapter 3 I stressed that professors think they teach the subjects they know. But students think professors do many things besides that. Professors come to a room filled with late adolescents and tell them things, that is, impart information. They then take the measure of what the students have heard and learned. They administer periodic examinations and grade the results, like eggs, with letters, even with plusses and minuses, no less. Strict logic might dictate that they thereby grade their own success as conveyors and purveyors of learned information, but that is a separate question.

It is hard to teach eighteen-year-olds, to ask them to think cogently for more than twenty seconds, to insist they answer a specific question and not some question no one has asked, to pick out purposeful from pointless remarks, and to demand that they learn from the teacher, not only from themselves — these do not add up to a prescription for public popularity or private ease. In the humanities I find it difficult to get students to take seriously what I have taught in a course. On finals some insist on writing things they knew or took for granted before they took the course and they ignore the argument of the course. Some write on subjects the course never took up, assuming as fact a wild range of misinformation and impression. And some get the point.

For some students, the professor may become far more than a teacher in a classroom. Students endowed with confidence and curiosity, who know what they want and are determined to get it, gain the legitimate power to transform the professor from enemy to opportunity. Seeking out the professor and attempting to make contact by expressing their ideas and so trying out on the professor the creations of their own design, these students create for themselves a resource of considerable worth. To other students, the professor may become a friend for professors are people, commonly parents. Many among them value friendship wherever they find it, among young as much as among peers. Students able to sustain relationships with adults, as well as professors open to friendship in age succeeding age, give to one another gifts beyond all valuation, an ever-renewed spring of life-nourishing love.

Some professors are more scholar than teacher, devoting long hours to research and writing. And this too is difficult — to think up new questions and to work out their answers, to write article after article, book after book. Not many professors actually open their ideas to public scrutiny by publishing articles and books for their colleagues' criticism. But many pretend to or promise that they will, and all profess to think it important to try, while hating the few who do so. Some professors give up the struggle of research once they are granted tenure. Some few continue to produce. And that means that not many continue to learn. To be a professor is to be a student all the time — a taxing vocation indeed.

The contradictions among types of professors flow from the diverse sorts of people who are drawn to this particular vocation. Some people love learning, taking ideas apart and putting them back together. If their interests center upon matters of academic learning, they aspire to become professors because they love precisely what professors do: learn and teach how interesting ideas work. These form a tiny proportion of the whole. Other people see in the life of a professor a protected refuge. Such people, unsure of themselves, seek the certainty of knowing one subject better than anyone else. Uncertain in relationships with others, they want not only to know the rules but to control them. So scholarship becomes an excuse not to relate ("too busy with my work"), and human encounter falls under rigid guidelines. For to read and think and write, people have to be on their own a great part of the day. If research institutes could absorb those who present both unusual intellectual strength and the capacity to work forever on their own and by themselves, then society as a whole would gain from their learning and not lose from the narcissism characteristic of a fair number of the great lonely learners.

Teaching Assistants

In most large universities, the professor addresses sizable numbers of students and in the nature of things cannot give proper attention to each individual student. But the professor will have assistants — normally, one for forty or fifty students. These assistants conduct discussion groups. They read exams. They maintain everyday contact with the undergraduates. In a fair number of universities, they are the only ones who will know students by name.

In the education of students, teaching assistants carry far more weight than anyone else. Why? Because the greater part of the person-to-person encounter, of which, ideally, education consists, is with the teaching assistants. The teachers whom I knew, who knew me and taught me as an undergraduate, were all teaching assistants. I retain close contact with some of them to this day. By contrast, not a single professor whom I knew as an undergraduate maintained any ties with me then or afterward. Quite to the contrary, college to me meant a handful of remarkably generous and devoted friends who were also my teachers. When students in larger universities reach the point at which they can frame ideas and offer them for public inspection, they address not professors, who rarely hear from students, but teaching assistants, who are paid to listen. These same people normally grade students' written work. Accordingly, at the two principal points at which students do not merely receive but also express thoughts, teaching assistants stand at the turning.

Let me spell out this fact, since I believe it is at the center of the education that the greater number of large universities provide. When you learn, you do two things. First, you receive; second, you try ideas out for yourself. You begin by acquiring information and learning how to use — manipulate — it, whether this is in lecture or in reading. (Normally, in higher education, it is through both media.) Then, if you are to benefit from what you read and hear, you must also attempt to make it your own. This you do by stating matters as you have heard or read them and also have reckoned with their meaning or point: how they work. Teaching assistants are there to listen.

Now in an ideal world, these teaching assistants would be junior professors, *assistant* professors in the true sense of the word. Like residents in a hospital, they would have completed their own education and begun to practice — that is, to teach. They would also enjoy close supervision of their actual teaching, and their capacities to read an examination and guide a student paper would flow from careful instruction and self-conscious example of the senior professor. They also would have a proper salary for their work. They would enjoy standing and position on account of it.

But in the real world, teaching assistants are graduate students, themselves in the earliest stages of their graduate education, many not even a year out of college. They are paid a pittance. They enjoy slight standing or prestige. Worse still, they are not supervised by senior professors, who rarely sit down and discuss the problems of teaching a given unit of a course, the difficulties students face in grasping a given idea, or the likely obstacles to grasping a stated proposition.

The education of graduate students provides for the future of learning in America, since today's graduate student may become tomorrow's great scholar and teacher. Parents of college freshmen like to think that their children are the focus of a university's teaching. But where there is a graduate school — and that means, at most of the important centers of higher learning — the professors' commitment focuses on their graduate students, who, in turn, take responsibility for undergraduates. For how graduate students are taught will define, for good or ill, how they themselves teach.

What does this mean for students and their parents? It means that when you visit a college or university, you should find out the extent to which senior professors seek an encounter in the classroom with small numbers of undergraduates. Are there seminars for undergraduates? How do you get into one? You should ask students how many professors know their names, and when they last talked to, and were heard by, someone more than a year or two older than themselves or the seniors. You should determine the normal size of the classes in which students hear lectures, and ask also the size and schedule of the meetings of discussion sections for those large courses. You will want to find out by what criteria teaching assistants are appointed — scholarly distinction or merely the need for financial support for graduate students. You should ask how the teaching assistants are supervised, the extent to which senior professors inquire into what their assistants are doing and review with them the pedagogical problems of a given topic or class. In all these ways you will assess for yourself the possibility that you will pay for a senior surgeon but end up having an intern remove your appendix.

In the end the particular student's own ambitions, his or her sense of self-confidence and intellectual purpose, will govern. If the critical issue is how you feel about yourself, what emerges from the interplay of teacher and student, the web of relationships spun on the loom of learning, then the small liberal arts college offers what you want. If the central purpose in university education is learning, and you find you can work on your own without sustaining relationships, then come to the cold, indifferent, but intellectually vital and rigorous classroom and laboratory of the great research university. On the whole, people choose well for themselves — or transfer.

Tenure

Before we leave the subject of who teaches, let me turn to the matter of tenure. This subject will affect your college career no matter where or what you study or with whom you study. What tenure means is that after a probationary period (usually six years) a college professor may apply for a lifelong appointment by the college or university at which he or she teaches. Unless the need for services should end, which is not common, the professor may look forward to a lifetime of employment. The professor is obligated at the most for only a few hours a week. The rest of the hours of the week are his or her own, to do with as the professor sees fit. Tenure generally appeals to people who suppose that security solves many problems. But it creates some too.

How shall we justify a system in which security takes precedence over achievement? There is a conflict of interest between students and their need to be taught, and teachers and their legitimate concern to keep their jobs. Tenure was created to protect those who needed protection, and it still serves that purpose. Professors ask for courage to speak the truth — but not at the cost of the food our children eat, the roof over our family's head. Tenure protects truth tellers; it allows for controversy and debate. But it also, of necessity, shelters everybody else.

If, as I have argued, to teach is to impart life, then when the teacher ceases to love the work of teaching, not for a moment but forever, the teacher should find some work to love again. Tenure prevents this. Few teachers have the courage to give up the security of a job for the freedom of having, not a job, but a choice. When the time comes to make a change, tenure forms a prison wall. Hanging around, the tenured teacher becomes cynical, bitter, jealous. Students no longer challenge, they only irritate. Fellow teachers no longer help and inspire; they only commiserate. The tiredness we all feel at the end of the year, the spiritual fatigue that tells us we have given our best and can give no more — these mark for some the beginning and middle of the year as well. And why? Because there is no choice. The present is known, the alternative frightening — especially for men and women in their forties, the point at which change is both still possible and also necessary.

I have observed over the years that the young scholar tends to run out of ideas and energy at the very point at which he or she attains tenure. For the first five or six years after graduate school, the young professor continues to read books and think about writing books. New ideas for courses percolate. The fact that there is a tenure decision down the pike also serves as inspiration to maintain the professional ambitions as teacher and even scholar with which the work began. After tenure, the truth comes out. It is at this point that the one scholar who, it turns out, really loved the work and lived for it, stands apart from the many scholars who loved and lost the love, or never really liked it all to begin with, but only the status. Some of these people find refuge in other activities, work on committees, or as department chairs, or even as assistant deans, associate provosts, and directors of this and that.

But the larger number do not. And they do little else. But they have tenure. It locks out life. It bars taking risks. It secures the prison — for those whose careers in all but form have ended. Students argue against tenure because they find themselves deprived of the promise of the young who care. Administrators argue against tenure because it ties their hands (as well they may have to be tied). But the true victim of tenure is the tenured.

Chapter Thirteen

Who Speaks for Colleges

Presidents

HE QUALITIES THAT MAKE A GOOD
teacher trouble a good administrator. The
pure and total freedom of encounter and expression demanded in our work with students presents problems for presidents and
provosts in their work. To run the great
institutions of society, they must have order. They need to nurture good will, a good name, generally good opinion, so people
will give the money needed to sustain the schools and colleges.
A well-run school is orderly. Life is predictable. Courses are
laid out so that there is a rough parity among classes.

In a president's or provost's job, to get along, he or she needs
to go along. Our skills as teachers are the skills of another sort
entirely. When we go along with our students as they are, unchanged, we do not get along in our work, we merely become
well liked. To serve effectively, we must be different from
presidents. To serve effectively, presidents must be different
from us.

What makes a good administrator is the capacity to do things
regularly and routinely, to keep things in hand and under
control. When deans plan budgets, they work a year in advance. They think quite properly about the ongoing life of the
institution they serve. They wish to keep the peace in the community they serve. Stability, order, good will, good organization — these are the marks of good administration. But mere
stability, order, good will, and good organization are insuf-
ficient for good teaching. I do not mean a classroom must
be disorderly. But ideas are disorderly. Intellectual life is full

115

of surprises and discoveries, I do not mean there should be any doubt that our courses begin somewhere and end up somewhere else; but a first-class course is one in which the conclusions are not predictable at the outset. Teaching is discovery and adventure, or it is merely relating information impersonally. Thus arises the conflict of interest between the good teacher and the good administrator.

Consider a particular fact, any particular fact. Telling the truth about that fact may not be good administration. But it will always be good teaching. When schools and colleges lose the reputation of freely teaching what is true to those capable of learning it, schools and colleges lose the public esteem and support they require. Then they turn to the community for bond issues and are turned down. In our own day we professors have compromised the three principal freedoms that make learning possible: (1) freedom to choose whom one finds qualified, (2) freedom to teach what one wants, (3) freedom to teach whoever is competent to learn. The damage done to the good name of universities in abridging those three freedoms accounts more than anything else for the present disesteem from which we all suffer. And we professors gave up those freedoms ourselves. We in universities stopped telling the truth about matters of solid achievement and demonstrated competence. No one gained, and everybody lost, when we academicians — professors and presidents — lied.

The mentality of bureaucrats stands at odds with what they administer in schools and colleges. It is one thing to write the book of rules and follow them when one is a captain in the army or a director of a government bureau or the manager of a corporate office. It is quite another to bring those same values into the schools. What makes a good teacher is not the ability to follow a book of rules, but the ability to criticize the rules and ask why they are there. That is not because criticism is what we do. It is because teaching is what we do. And to teach, we must bring to life our students' and our own capacity for response, for thought and reflection — and that means, to criticize.

Bureaucracies keep things going through public relations. Teachers ask embarrassing questions. Clerks and administrators pass out news releases to reporters. Teachers shrug their shoulders and tell the truth — even to reporters. The president of a university wants everyone to think well of the university. The professor in that university wants everyone to think. The president is right for corporations, but not for universities. The professor affirms life — the vitality of ideas, the good health of argument and controversy.

Schools and colleges are not well served by dissimulation. They are not preserved by public relations. Schools and colleges are strong enough to bear true witness, even about education. They are not fragile, to be protected by lies. They are strong and essential, the bone of our bone, the life blood of our society. The reputation of the schools and colleges does not rest upon the discretion of liars in public relations. It rests upon the achievement of teachers. Admit to the problems and people will believe us. Gloss them over and they will lose faith. We teachers stand before our students to wake them up to what they can be. When we do our work, people will respect and sustain us. When we do not do our work, people will not believe in us, no matter what the public relations directors, alumni magazine editors, presidents, and board chairmen may say.

This brings me to presidents in particular. Once upon a time, the president of a university became governor of his state, and, a few years later, president of the United States. That was Woodrow Wilson, who went from Princeton to Trenton to Washington. When I was a boy in Connecticut, presidents of Yale University regularly came under discussion as possible Senate candidates. People turned to college presidents for their opinions on a vast range of subjects, as today they turn to TV personalities (or controversial professors). More influential than politics in the framing of cultural concerns and values of the country, college presidents took a vigorous part. They made speeches about ideas, won attention for issues of the intellect, spoke out on questions of higher education.

The presidency of a university was a bully pulpit, and great women and men used it. They furthermore imposed their views of what their universities should do, leading the faculty to effect substantial changes in curriculum and in the organization of education. They were figures of controversy and they thrived on it. College presidents created universities, like Abram Sachar of Brandeis. College presidents transformed universities, like Henry Wriston and then Barnaby Keeney at Brown. In the more distant past, the influence of presidents such as James Conant of Harvard, Robert Hutchins at Chicago, and Nicholas Murray Butler at Columbia, and the standing of the presidents of the great state universities of Michigan, Illinois, Wisconsin, constituted formative forces in the definition of America. They had a purpose and a program. And, by the way, college presidents raised money. Today college presidents only raise money. There is no vision, no center, no goal — just the budget.

The 1960s and 1970s promised a call to greatness, but in those years the timid administrators survived, the great educators —Clark Kerr of California is the best example — perished from the campus. In scurrying for security in the face of upheaval and chaos, boards of trustees let college presidencies fall into the hands of people who promised little more than compromise to effect their own surival and, with it, the survival of their college. But survival for what? If survivors themselves cannot tell you, then what have they survived? In the aftermath of the revolution of a decade and a half ago, a new formalism replaced the old.

The public imagines that the college president leads, presides, sets standards, and provides an example and a model for students and teachers alike. But these days the college president rarely leads as the educator that people rightly expect the president to be. The college president is interchangeable with other corporate presidents (as in the case of Dartmouth). Why? Good administration applies equally to government, industry, and the academic world. What that means is that there is no longer a career of educational leadership reaching the climax in a presidency of a college in particular.

The president can be president of anything, which is another way of saying that the president of a college is nothing in particular.

As a result, we do not live in the age of great university presidents who give leadership to education in particular. The most recent age of great university presidencies began in 1945 and ended in 1970. We live in the age of effective and successful administrators who pay bills. Presidents tend to bow out of important discussions of purpose and meaning in education — like rich, absentee parents. It is probably the way things have to be. But colleges lose the opportunity of leadership. Without vision the people perish. Without presidents who stand for something to do with learning, universities and colleges pay their bills on time, but they go nowhere, lacking all direction and purpose. Leadership depends upon opportunity, and the president has that opportunity. And great leaders create their opportunities.

College freshmen give the gift of believing in the college of their choice. They seek models, new beginnings for themselves, paths to a worthwhile future. Above all they look for striking leadership, for examples of what they may become, for someone to say, through example more than through word, "Follow me! After me! To life!" What they find, in contrast to what they seek, is at best gray competence.

Presidents should impart vision and provide a view of the whole. By reason of their office, they should speak of the great and general purposes of the college, the hope it extends to its students, the high duties it demands of its professors. The president has the power not to make things work — that is the task of the professors — but to make things work together. In a word, the college president should define the ideals of the college, lead, envision the whole, and aim to attain it.

In general, that is not what college presidents do, and it is not even what they try to do. They should lead, but they administer. They should see a vision of the whole, but they worry instead about the budgets of the parts. Success for them is measured in dollars, and the "real world" imposes its values on their daily work. Accordingly, success depends not on learning — education and scholarship — but upon other things entirely. Others, in other offices of the university, could surely carry out these practical tasks quite well. For instance, no one today imagines that a college president should manage the college's investments. There is a specialist for that. Well and good, but then why should the president serve as primary figure in "development" (which means fund raising)? The president should do what no one else can do, what no other position in the university permits one to do, and that is, lead, inspire, call forth greatness, recognize achievement, give a model for learning in community that the college is meant to embody. I cannot think of any college president today who would attempt such a definition of his or her presidency. In consequence university presidents rarely attain eminence in education and often are not educators at all. As I said, industry, business, government, and now universities trade leaders among one another. The *what* matters less than the *how*.

To the trustees universities are interchangeable with corporations, government offices, and factories. The trustees are wrong. Colleges demand leadership particular to their tasks. Education produces something more fundamental to society than does industry, government, or business. Colleges need educators for their leaders. A great college president is great in ways different from a great industrialist, banker, or bureaucrat. Our bottom line reads differently. We pay our dividends in human lives. Our budgets are balanced in books and in great ideas and ideals.

You may say, "Yes, but you do have to pay the bills." True enough. But you pay the bills in order to get something worth having. More important than paying the bills is educating the students and nurturing learning. If the president does not know what education is, cannot use the position of prominence and power that he or she holds in such a way that the college becomes more vital, more effective, who needs a president? Why not hand over the presidency to the fund-raising office or to the business administrator, and the university to other hands entirely? Today higher education can point to few examples of true greatness — I mean, those who aspire to greatness of heart and mind and spirit. That is why we need great men and women to set an example, to lead universities and to make them places of greatness. To settle for people who can raise a lot of money hands the future over to amiable nonentities who have no clear idea of what they wish to do with their own success. In the end it is a kind of self-celebration and we end up with the status quo, in concrete.

Do I sound disappointed? Is this a mere diatribe? You bet. I was once interviewed for a college presidency. Having declared myself the least qualified person the trustees could uncover, I explained why: "You people want a president to raise money. I want to be a president who walks around the campus, smiles a lot, and says wise things to people." That mysterious pronouncement closed the interview, though the conversation persisted for two hours afterward. I never heard from those people again, but I have thought about the matter a great deal.

Why am I so disappointed at the state of the university presidency? Because I see the promise and the hope of the office, and because I believe that, more than any other, the institution headed by the office shapes the future of America. We are not talking about the person in charge of an institution that does not settle important questions. We are talking about leadership that shapes coming generations of young Americans. Few presidents today have important views on education or offer a cogent philosophy of what a university does. Power without purpose proves as perilous in college presidents as in U.S. presidents. But more is at stake in college: the future of young women and men. For presidents without goals pass in a few years, but the effects of an aimless education for students in those same four or five years last a lifetime.

Which weighs more — an unbalanced budget or a wasted life? And how shall we balance the value of a balanced budget against the cost of a generation deprived of vision and left without challenges of greatness? The young people will follow a leader; the campus requires leaders. The college presidency should be a place for great women and men to speak out in important ways about important matters of heart and mind and spirit. By that criterion, that presidency today stands empty. It is like the Irish churches after Cromwell. Where God was served, the choirs stood bare and ruined, the roof open to the skies, the walls crumbling. After the victory over the universities by administrators, the mind survives empty of meaning — all for want of great presidents, men and women of great hearts and high hopes.

Chapter Fourteen

Everyone Teaches
in a Community of Learning

RESIDENTS, DEANS, PROVOSTS, AND PRO-
fessors take for granted that universities are
centers of higher learning. But universities
are places in which young people go from
adolescence to maturity while engaged in
higher learning — in that order. The students
spend only part of their time in the classroom, library, or lab.
They spend much of their time in the dining halls and dormi-
tories, on the sports fields, and socializing with one another.
In relation to the things that matter to students, what professors do is useful but not critical. Many students worry about
whether they are liked. We want them to be learned. Many
want to know that they are attractive to the opposite sex. We
care that they think clearly. They often entertain fears about
their future, and we listen to the clarity of their argument
and the precision of their reasoning. A gap separates the purveyors of higher education from the consumers.

There is only one way to bridge the gap, and that is by trans-
forming colleges and universities into places in which everyone undertakes both to teach and to learn. In a community
of learning, exchanges of insight and even of information will
take place in each transaction and encounter. In the community of learning formed by a college, the focus of education is
the undergraduate; the object of education is the student's
growth to maturity in mind and in heart. So we teach students,
but students by definition educate us professors in our responsibilities. For professors in particular, the students teach
teaching. They respond to what we say and do. If we succeed,

123

we know it in their powers of heart and mind. When we fail, we see it in their confusion and doubt. I have never completed a semester without totaling up the wins and the losses, and I never win them all. I'm always glad simply to have made a difference.

Many other sorts of officials and officers may define the character of a college or university. For example, the way in which secretaries conduct themselves may teach lessons about life more immediate and more telling than anything professors say. Why are secretaries central? Because, as soon as students come to meet professors or teaching assistants, they walk through the door of an office and confront a person in charge. That person is not a professor or a teaching assistant and may not have an academic degree. Yet the secretary guards the door and says to this one, "Yes, go in," and to that one, "No, the professor is 'too busy.'" The secretary answers the phone, takes the messages, transacts much of the business of professors when they deal not only with students but also with the rest of the university's management, not to mention the outside world.

The way the details of department life are carried on is all important to students. How so? If secretaries are cordial and friendly, they create a setting in which students rightly feel respected and important. If they are cold and unresponsive, they create a framework in which students rightly feel abused and disregarded. Since the student is at the center of the university, the principal reason for its being, the way the students are treated signals the prevailing atmosphere of the university, defining what it is like to be a student there. In this regard, the secretary plays a more critical part in the life of the university, so far as students' understanding is concerned, than many people who appear to outsiders to be more important.

Many others meet students. The majority of these members of the management and service staff of the university are not academicians. But in the nature of what they do, they always are teachers. They have a life beyond the university's walls and sometimes students come to understand that. Yet they invariably teach students the most important lesson the university imparts: how much we care for you, the student. When library employees try to accommodate students' interests and help them make use of the books, when cafeteria workers, lab assistants, and custodial workers befriend the students and take an interest in their lives, then the entire university becomes a happy community. But when the basic attitude of the staff expresses disdain, when people do not try to accommodate the students and solve their problems, then the university contradicts its purpose. The students receive the wordless lesson that human concerns and reason take second place, and the convenience of the autocracy — and even a dean of housing may play the part of autocrat — is paramount.

Universities ought to carry out the policy that education happens everywhere and all the time. Hence clear operating routines should express the policy that we are here to solve the students' problems as best we can, to make them happy, to accommodate their wishes so far as we can. This we do by an appeal to reason and good sense, by a systematic and consistent refusal to say no when there is any possibility of saying yes. The world at large accommodates peoples' whims and allows people in authority — however trivial — to show the world how they feel this morning. We can do very little about the grouchy bus driver who closes the door in our face. We cannot get back at the rude salesperson, the needlessly officious guard or customs inspector, the one who never smiles, the one who never says yes. But in a university we can do a great deal to cultivate a friendly spirit, an attitude of solicitous concern for students and all people.

That does not mean we teach only by saying yes. It does mean that we teach courtesy by trying to be courteous, just as much as we teach clear expression by trying to say things clearly. Our example need not replicate the world beyond our gates. For we stand for reasonable discourse and the power of argument to change minds. We demonstrate what we mean to teach not merely in the classroom argument but also in the use of rational discourse and reasonable modes of persuasion in every corner of the campus.

Assistant deans come in many shapes and sizes. Outside of the classroom, they are the university officials students are most likely to know. Indeed, students will know them better than they know professors. The students do not choose their own rooms and roommates, but someone assigns them; students do not maintain their own records, but someone oversees them; they do not come and go without paying tuition and receiving credits and going through a considerable number of formalities. Students moreover have problems of which the professor remains ignorant. They go to deans of students, to health services, and to others as important in the welfare of the undergraduates as the professor. Universities, moreover, offer a broad range of extracurricular, but educationally vital, activities, such as student unions, bookstores, discussion facilities, clubs and organizations, and publications of all kinds. These do not happen by themselves. Deans of student life nurture them and guide them, while preserving students' freedom to make of them what they will.

Such people as secretaries, food service employees, library workers, physicians, nurses, librarians, deans, coaches, and guards play a vital and intimate role in the life of the student and of the college. In fact students who play sports learn more from coaches than from others, fall more under their influence and model than under the spell of even the most brilliant lecturer. The life of the students is lived for a dozen hours a week in the classroom, and for 156 hours a week on the campus and beyond the classroom. That is why secretaries, the maintenance staff, library specialists, the university's police force, assistant deans, associate provosts, and all the others who run part of the university must have one ability above all others: the ability to teach, to serve as an example. We shall never attain perfection, but we can always try to overcome our incapacity. Just as there must be a standard of reason in the classroom, so there should be a policy of accommodation and good will outside it. Let the exceptions to the norm testify that in life at large, it is normal to be nice. Let me now offer some details on how to assess this aspect of a college.

When you visit a campus, look into three specific areas. First, are students happy with the health center and related services? If they are sick, do the doctors and nurses treat them with respect? What happens in a crisis, whether psychological or medical? How effective are the responses? Second, can students see deans and professors readily and easily, or are offices tightly closed to them? Third, are there enough resources to deal with the many problems a student will face? Be prepared to ask the students specific questions about all three areas. You will probably not learn much about the health services, since crises are relatively few on campus. But do pose questions and listen to the answers. They will tell you how comfortable the students are with the school's facilities. You will learn far more about deans and other officers. Do students find it easy to get an appointment? Are there enough deans so that all students get the attention they need? Is there a broad variety of deans, covering diverse special tasks, so that a single dean can pay adequate attention to a few specific responsibilities? As you are learning about the deans, you will also be learning about the school's resources. If there are housing problems, do people take them seriously? If a student has to change a room, does someone care? When there are problems with a tuition payment or a meal contract, does someone take charge and solve the problem? Or do students find themselves unable to conduct their business rapidly and efficiently?

These are the sorts of questions that will lead parents and prospective students into the everyday reality created by the support staff of the college or university. If you ask general questions, you will come away with generalizations — and happy lies. If you ask students whether they are happy, they will answer that they are. But if you ask students what substantial problem they faced outside the classroom, and how they found help in solving that problem, you will learn specific and important information about the conduct of life at that college.

My impression is that colleges and universities, on the whole, do a first-rate job of tending to the extracurricular and noncurricular lives of their students. But any prospective car buyer who does not inquire into the working of the service department deserves to buy a lemon, and whoever does not know in advance whether and how a college's entire system of deans and directors does its work will find out at a not-very-fortunate hour.

Part Three

What Really Happens in College

Chapter Fifteen

Freshman Bliss, Sophomore Slump

J UST LIKE THE BONES OF "DEM BONES . . . ," so the senior year of high school is attached to the freshman year of college, and the freshman year of college is attached to the sophomore year of college. The true cut-off point comes at the end of the sophomore year and the beginning of the junior year. Let's treat the sophomore and freshman years together, since they form a single continuous sequence of educational experience and emotional response.

To begin with, let me tell a brief story to illustrate what I said earlier about high school seniors. Once upon a time there was a high school senior. He worked hard and got decent grades, until the first semester of the senior year. Then he filled out his college applications and retired. The rest of his senior year in high school he griped and complained. But he did very little schoolwork. He gave up his music lessons. He stopped studying. He barely survived. On the strength of three and a half years of high school grades, he got into the University of Chicago. He did not want to go to his high school graduation. He went wearing a T-shirt and jeans. He did not want his parents to attend. After the summer, and before he went off to Chicago, what happened? He got a calculus book and a tutor, and in five weeks he completed the entire first semester math course that he would have to take at the University of Chicago. He hoped to qualify for the second semester course, right at the outset. That senior is my first son, who I always thought was an average, reasonably decent student. And there is a moral to this tale.

Schoolwork that seemed a waste of time in the final months of high school suddenly merits conviction and commitment in the first days of college. The glorious moment of the opening of freshman year brings sunshine where there was gloom, hope where there was despair, belief in education, in a limitless future, where there had been nothing but boredom and surrender. The happiest moment on a college campus is the day the freshmen arrive and the following week or two. From that point forward, nothing seems beyond reach. Endless possibilities open up. Would that we could find the way to keep alive that moment of rebirth and renewal. But the miracle of the opening week depends upon a circumstance that comes only a few times in any person's lifetime: the hour of new beginnings, fresh chances. People still bring to wherever they go the same weaknesses and strengths, fears and hopes. That does not mean the moment of renewal does not matter. It matters very much, like the marriage rite. It gives the college a chance that high school (through no fault of its own) never had.

But a slump surely follows. Why? Because no one can live life on so high a pitch of hope. Everyone comes back to an accurate assessment of how things really are. Learning still demands work. Teachers still drone on. Education does not take place at life's highs, though it surely leads to the high places of the good life of mind and heart. So after a few weeks of sustaining unreal expectation, students return to earth. They call it the freshman blues, or it may be sophomore slump; it may last for half a year or a year. The single most common cause of students' giving up college, I think, lies here: the death of hope that no one could keep alive. People cannot sustain the unreal expectation of change accomplished without anguish and learning without effort. But the concern now is not with the ones who leave. It is with those who remain.

What is to be done to deal with the freshman's move from bliss to blues, and the sophomore's slump from the heights of noble goals to the depths of disappointment, first of all with themselves? What is to be done, indeed! We must deal, not with the symptoms, but with the cause of the disease. The symptom is excessive hope followed by depression, blues, slump. The cause is twofold: first comes the failure of the students; second, and more serious, comes the failure of the college professors.

How do the colleges fail? The answer derives from how they succeed. Some universities and many good colleges propose to offer freshmen and sophomores seminars to stimulate the students into more adventures at learning as discovery and to counteract the effect of several lecture courses. Schools organize small freshman classes with senior professors. These schools move sophomores rapidly into courses that work as seminars, that is, as occasions for experiment, discovery, and testing. In these schools freshmen and sophomores fare better, for they are clearly being drawn into the best the college has to offer. And this offers us a clue to the freshman blues and the sophomore slump. Whether or not the freshmen go from bliss to blues may depend on whether the freshmen truly leave high school when they reach college. When sophomores slump, it may be that they slide to the level of the curriculum, with its depths of boredom.

Let us consider this possibility from another angle. Studies indicate that students spend most of their class time listening to a professor. They enjoy slight opportunity to respond and frame their own ideas. I know the temptation to blather. When I teach, I always have to remind myself that I am never so interesting to others as I find myself to be. Now if you were in a classroom in which your job was to sit and take notes, would you not find it comfortable to slump down in your chair and relax? And what is sophomore slump, if not emotional equivalent to the posture in the classroom?

Once students recognize the origins of the blues and the slump, they can protect themselves from them. This they can do (depending on the resources of their college or university) by enrolling in small courses in preference to large ones; by studying with more effective teachers, who may teach less popular subjects, rather than with ineffective teachers blabbing at a captive audience; by exploring new subjects not studied in high school, instead of familiar subjects studied at merely a higher level than in high school. These three criteria for selecting the freshman and sophomore years' courses, which I noted earlier, run counter to the conventions of the day. Freshmen normally take more of what they already have taken. They ordinarily judge a course by the subject matter, rather than by the teacher. They therefore find themselves in the curse of higher education, the enormous freshman course, rather than the smaller upper class course. So they are talked at for a year or two and end up passive, sullen, bored. Who would not be!

Students fail to learn not only because of their inexperience in choosing their courses. They also fail because of their wholly unrealistic assessment of what to expect in college. What they do find is a world much more different from home than they expected or realized at first. The demands exceed anything the students have formerly met. The freedoms prove to be without precedent in the students' lives. The way through the morass of uncertainty and insecurity commonly lies through familiar paths, tested responses.

I find it difficult, for example, to engage students in the serious search for the right courses, and this is in a university in which students are completely free to choose what they like without faculty interference. Students want pretty much what they have had, or they choose what they think their future professional school or calling demands. It is one thing for a premedical student to take biology. It is quite another for a premedical student not to take history. It is one thing for a prelaw student to elect courses in political science. It is quite another for a prelaw student to avoid mathematics or physics. Worse still, as I suggested, is the student who brings English, history, chemistry, mathematics, and French from high school and enrolls in advanced courses in exactly the same subjects. When students discover the subjects that in high school they did not know existed, their education in college begins: philosophy, sociology, anthropology, education, the academic study in religion, economics, or the new humanities,

Near Eastern or women's studies, or South Asian, Chicano, Judaic, or black studies, and the like.

Students not only avoid exercising that freedom of choice that they come to college to gain. Some also do not come to grips with the new responsibility they bear for themselves. Instead of standing up and coming to decisions on their own, they find a new tyrannical peer group to replace the one they left behind in high school. They run in packs for a semester or a year, only slowly breaking off into smaller groups of friends, people with common interests. Actively placing upon themselves the restraints of peer pressure that, by the senior year, they will scarcely recognize, the freshmen as well as a fair number of sophomores substitute for uncertainty and insecurity a pattern they later on must and will break. People do not live their lives in packs. In the things that count they do not follow the pressures of others. But freshmen do. The radical change in educational and social situation that college presents thus demands growth, a coming outward and a taking of risks. But what comes forth not uncommonly is what has worked in the past.

The real crisis of the freshman and sophomore years is not limited to education and the intellect. Indeed, many beginning students do far better with their courses than with their lives outside class. The confrontation with freedom, the need to make one's own decisions in place of rebelling against parental choices, the insecurity of living life on one's own — these generate both the bliss and the blues. I hear (but I can't verify it) that many freshmen gain weight — ten pounds on the average — in their first months in college simply because, eating on their own, they choose the wrong foods and throw off the restraints of home. Whether or not that is so, it surely symbolizes other problems. Leaving home is hard. It also is necessary. And, in our society, young people tend to leave home after high school. Some go into the army; others take full-time jobs; half go to college or a university.

When you realize that unreal expectations and inappropriate disappointment constitute responses to the same, essentially nonacademic crisis of life, you grasp what colleges can, and cannot, do for their students. They can provide delightful circumstances in which to grow up. They can offer wise counsel and attractive models. They cannot bear the pain of growing, and they cannot do the work of maturing. So far as learning can help people to grow and mature, colleges and universities present a splendid opportunity to precisely the age group that is at hand. So far as people in the end have to make the passage on their own, all we can do is hope — and pray.

Chapter Sixteen

Why Juniors Leave School
(and Junior Year Abroad)

IRST, LET ME SAY WHAT I MEAN BY A junior. A junior is a student who has completed one half of the degree requirements, that is, someone contemplating the world at the end of the sophomore year. A junior by spring of the junior year sees things very differently. What happens after the end of two years, but before the end of the third? Three things.

First, the student reaches a plateau in learning, having mastered the challenges of the freshman year and early part of the sophomore year, but not having attained the heights of mastery of a subject, the satisfaction of solid achievement.

Second, the student has to find a major of some kind. That means defining himself or herself.

Third, the student gets terribly tired, with far too much ahead, yet a great deal behind.

The frame of mind of the student at the end of the sophomore year finds definition in the set of questions to be answered, in most universities, pretty much at that very moment. For two years the university commonly tells the students what to take, with requirements of various kinds intended to lead the students (or drag them) through the principal parts of the curriculum. Consequently, students learn a little bit about a lot of subjects. They also feel they control little about their own educations, since they are told what to take, what to study. So the first two years perpetuate the conditions students know in high school. How so? First, they study many of the same subjects. Second, they study in much the same way. Therefore, college by this point proves a disappointment. It is really just a fifth and sixth year of high school (as in some foreign countries, there is a fifth and sixth year of high school). True, the student has survived the freshman year, but the excitement and hope of that heady season have faded. What is left is more of the same, alongside exhaustion.

Yet at that very moment of withdrawal and depression, students confront a new demand: They are told to choose. In a great many colleges and universities, during the later part of the sophomore year and the early part of the junior year, students must decide on their major. What this means is that they have to choose how they wish to identify themselves. They are now going to fall into classifications: a history major, a science major, with all that those classifications add to their identities as people. (For everyone "knows" what sociologists or mathematicians or engineers are like.) The major in my view creates more problems that it solves. True, the major ensures that students learn something about one subject in depth. But it also limits students, imposes upon them an identification they have not framed for themselves, precipitates a crisis of choice for which, in the circumstances of the imposed curriculum, they are not wholly prepared.

At the end of the sophomore year, moreover, students look back on a measure of achievement. After all, they have worked hard and learned much. With their passing or honor grades, they know they can do the work. The uncertainty of the freshman year is over. The intellectual challenges of the junior and senior years, with their advanced courses, small and more specialized seminars, more intimate contact with faculty members, have not yet begun. Students look back on what they have achieved, but they cannot fail to see all that lies ahead. And the prospect of the future tires them.

The student no longer expects the future to be exciting or rewarding, yet in most universities the junior year promises challenges that freshmen and sophomores scarcely imagine. Upon the foundations of elementary or introductory courses, the professors build advanced studies, in which students see how knowledge comes about. Students begin to grasp that there are levels and layers of learning. Some things do come before others. Now, at last, they enter the higher ranges of knowledge. What they find when they get there is the realm that professors truly inhabit. That is, learning men and women ask hard questions. Real learners follow up on curiosity. Good students weigh alternatives and explore the unthinkable. Knowledge is not fixed, and facts are few. All things become part of a game of learning, a sport of endless possibilities.

The frontiers of knowledge lie far above the beginnings of study, and to reach that height people have to climb. To get to the areas we really do not know, we have to pass through a long expanse of known territory. So in those advanced courses, students cease merely to learn more about what they already know. Like graduate students they come to join the craftsman as apprentice, the master as neophyte. Studying is no longer a burden. It becomes a quest. Not all, not even many, students reach and cross the frontiers of learning, but some do, and they generally do so in their junior and senior years. They then set the style, define the frame of mind, for many others. Learning becomes no longer a burden alone but also a joy and an engagement of discovery.

How do students cope with the predicament of the junior year? Some choose the moment to take a year off entirely. (Indeed, some tell themselves they leave for a year when they leave for good.) Taking a year off seems to me a mature and wholly wise decision. Students who work for a year, either before they come to college or after completing a year or two of study, learn lessons college cannot teach. They know that nothing comes for nothing. Hard work and achievement do not represent a favor you do for someone else or even for yourself, but an obligation, a requirement of life. Accordingly, when these students come back, they tend to appreciate much that they took for granted, like an act of courtesy from a professor, interest in their work on the part of teachers and fellow students, freedom to do one's work how one chooses — in all, the special privileges of the academic setting. They also come back to us with clearer goals for themselves, and a more accurate understanding of what they do well and what they do not find interesting after all. They are larger, richer, more interesting people. With a whole set of new questions and insights, they find their studies more relevant; their act of learning ceases to exhibit a passive and submissive quality. They are adults. That year has made the difference. The junior and senior years ahead bring joy and fulfillment, a climax to a great adventure in life.

Another group of students chooses to spend junior year overseas, or at some other university in America, or to transfer to another university altogether. The ones who go abroad invariably find for themselves a pleasant niche; they may learn a foreign language. They meet new people. They "have new experiences" (a phrase so vague I cannot say just what it means). In my view the only consistent achievement of the junior year abroad will be that the student has been abroad. Beyond that I can predict nothing.

Overseas programs vary wildly from one another. Few make the demands that rigorous academic programs in this country do. Few select among applicants. Most admit everybody. Few pay a great deal of attention to our students or know or care what sort of teaching works for Americans, and what does not. Few view the foreign student as part of their solemn educational responsibility. Many are glad to have only their money in tuition. Consequently, among the ways in which people can endure fraud and outright larceny in educational settings, chief among them is the overseas university's program for foreign students. I need hardly hasten to point to exceptions; there are always exceptions. But the rule is that the overseas university serves — like college itself — as a very expensive baby sitter. The important exception comes, not with the university, but with the American student. The one who goes abroad with a clear purpose, knowing precisely what he or she wishes to learn, intelligently uses that year. For the foreign city is a classroom in a foreign culture, and natural learning fills the waking hours. Accordingly, the many who go abroad for a long vacation find in their company a few who learn. My advice is to view with considerable skepticism the junior year abroad. Both the foreign university and the American student conspire in making an easy life. But where American universities themselves organize and run overseas programs, the picture is much brighter. Then our standards of education, our procedures for teaching, take over, and students gain the benefit of overseas study while not losing the advantage of higher American expectations in the classroom and laboratory.

Some students decide to change universities during this year. I cannot think of a braver or bolder idea. European university students move from place to place, going to the great professor in one subject after another. What if, in America, students built their educations by studying one subject with the great teacher in one college, then moving on to a different subject with an equally great teacher somewhere else? What if they studied the same subject with two great professors, with opposite views on every point? I cannot think of a more stimulating or interesting mode of learning. It seems obvious that when students have reached the end of the opportunities — so far as they grasp them — in one place, they do well to go on to some other. Furthermore, if students have made a mistake in their original choice of a college, they either persist in the mistake or correct it. It is better to recognize an error, learn its lessons, and move on — in life as much as learning. For these to me self-evident reasons, I think every sophomore should ask why he or she chooses to stay in college, and in that particular college, on the occasion of completing the sophomore year.

The junior year presents a diverse set of solutions to a single problem. Students have traveled far, with far to go. Some drop out. Some go abroad. Some switch universities. The only error is to persist in error. Students who trudge onward because parents insist learn all the wrong lessons about life. Those who confront the challenge of boredom, who recognize their own yearnings for change, or who focus upon a new world of language and culture and vision — these turn the junior year into the climax of their college education. Nor should we forget that a sizable majority of college students successfully move upward into the major and the advanced courses of the curriculum. The main point is only that after two years students not stand still.

Chapter Seventeen

Seniors

Cynics with Misty Eyes

 HE SENIOR CLASS POLL ASKS PROSPEC-
tive graduates whether they are glad they
came to the college they are about to leave.
If you poll the seniors in March, 95 percent
of them will say no. If you poll them in May,
95 percent of them will say yes. So much for
our success in imparting a sense of self-consciousness, of place
and the relativities of season and sentiment.

Why are seniors cynics?

Let us start with seniors in high school. When high school
students have completed their college applications and have
dispatched their fall semester grades, they retire. They reject
everything they have done for three and a half years, declaring themselves exempt from life. Learning no longer matters;
it is an empty and formal exercise. Learning is time serving;
the classroom is a fraud. Living is a sequence of time-filling
excuses: television, pickup basketball games, lying around and
shooting the breeze. What has happened? The pressure to
achieve and even to excel is gone. Colleges will make their
decisions. The students' part of the transaction has reached
its conclusion. There is nothing more to be done. So they do
nothing.

The cynicism of the high school senior proves fragile. It
quickly gives way to eagerness about what lies ahead. When
the colleges respond and the students gain admission to some
reasonably acceptable school, they begin to look forward, to
renew ambition, to want to accomplish something with their

time and with their lives. True, they continue to look backward with, at best, disdain. The high school they endured must be the worst in America, the teachers empty-headed, the curriculum a waste of time, the whole experience a wasteland. That is part of the pain of leaving — rejection and disdain for what one must give up anyway. It is easier to leave a place we claim to hate than one we admit we love. The whole panoply of timing and emotion combines to impose a separation, a distance, between students and the school they have known for four years — known, accepted as pretty much how things are and should be, and now must leave. It is like a death or a divorce, this breaking of ties. The result is that six months of life go down the tubes.

College seniors relive the crisis of the final semester of high school. But the stakes are higher, the issues more acute. For now the students face outward, toward the end of their student years altogether. They no longer look forward to more of the same; now they look forward to an unknown. Some go on to professional school — law, medicine, business, journalism. A very few go on to graduate school in the arts and sciences. Most go out to make a living — and to begin to make a life for themselves on their own.

How tender, how sweet, how frightening that month of May, when everything is done, but the world is yet unborn, the last term of pregnancy for a life about to begin. And yet how tense. And therein lies the key to the conflicting emotions of the senior year, particularly at the end. On the one side, the student looks back with a certain fondness. This one I will miss. That book I still remember. The student takes for granted that when he or she moves on, something here will remain the same. Students grow older, professors will endure as they always were, in permanent dotage. I leave, the buildings stay, the people stay. The college becomes a permanent beacon as the student embarks on an uncertain journey.

True enough, but uncertainty remains. In their natural unease before an unknown tomorrow, the students look backward and inward. They turn in against themselves, interpreting their unease to mean incompetence. They see themselves as too slight, too small, for what lies ahead. They have not yet had the experience of succeeding, or at least surviving, as adults. What their parents and older brothers and sisters have succeeded in doing — leaving college, getting and holding a job, forming permanent relationships of work and love — they have not yet done. They do not know whether or not they can do these things. So they are uneasy. They look backward at their four years of college, and in that nervous moment of departure, they call into question the value of what they have done. But, of course, in some people's minds, it is hard to admit to failure. Others fail *them*. For many of us, our faults are not commonly our own. They are caused by others. So here, too, the college has failed. If only it had done a good job of education, I would be more and better than I am. I feel small and weak and incapable, so I have *been* failed. That is why, in a poll in late winter, so many seniors will tell you they wish they had gone somewhere else.

But winter passes. By late spring, students realize that the path successfully walked by so many before them lies open to them too. They can make it on their own. And their college years have not proved so completely a waste as they thought. There were the experiences of growth and maturing. And some of these even took place in the classroom, library, laboratory, sports field, the settings of formal education and disciplined work of learning and maturing. So it was not so great, but it also was not so bad. That is, it was a replica of the world as it really is, never so awful as we fear, never so wonderful as we hope. Seniors are cynics. But when they march in graduation processions, it is with tears in their eyes.

Chapter Eighteen

Sex

EX? IN A BOOK ON EDUCATION? WHEN I told my undergraduates I was writing this book and could not think of a title, their first proposal, made unanimously, was "Sex and the Single Student." It was spontaneous, and no one offered anything else. I said, "Yes, but it's a book about higher education — the classroom, not the bedroom." But the students were right, and I was wrong. If I claim that students grow up in colleges and universities, then I cannot omit sex. If, further, I allege that how students feel affects what they learn, if I claim that higher education takes place throughout the whole week, not only in the twelve hours spent in the classroom, then I have no choice.

It's difficult for nonexperts to write on such subjects. What do I have to tell you, when I find it difficult (like many parents) to say anything about sex to my sons and daughters? Yet we teach in whatever we do, whether as parents or as professors, and I expect my children have learned more from me than I thought to teach them.

Let me offer three simple rules.

First, sex really is on our minds a great deal of the time. Instead of denying it, use that fact in affirming yourself. A fair number of adolescents pretend that if they don't bother "it," "it" won't bother them. But our personalities, our relationships, our way of life, derive definition from our sexual identities. Male and female were re-created. Each of us perceives the world more in the light of our sex than in the aspect of age or regional or ethnic origin (to name three important determinants). We express ourselves at least as much in how we respond to our sexual personality as we do in how we eat a meal or walk down the street or organize our everyday lives.

Second, since sex does matter, we may have to try to define ourselves in response to its realities, its demands and uncertainties. Despite much talk about sexual revolutions, my impression is that more students fear sex than play around. They hope to postpone relating to the opposite sex at all, thinking that that is for after college, for some other life. That does not mean they do not go through the motions of physical sexual relationships; some do. It means that they do not enter into real relationships with the opposite sex. They do not really know or develop a fondness for, an understanding of, a particular person of the opposite sex.

Yet in life we all need a long-term and deep relationship with another person, ordinarily someone of the opposite sex. It is part of the continuity of life that men relate to their mothers and their wives, and in those patterns (or the opposite) to other women (including their daughters), and women relate to their fathers and their husbands, and in those patterns to their sons and other men.

In contrast to high school, college life permits casual acquaintance, leading even to friendship, with people different from ourselves, even with those of the opposite sex. So if late adolescence is a time of uncertainty, it also presents the chance to experiment. And one important area of change and growth lies beyond the boundaries of established single-sex relationships. For in some ways it really is easier for boys to relate to boys, and girls to girls — easier, less threatening, more casual. But a full life demands the opposite — the effort and commitment that reach full expression in sex, at the right time and with the right person.

Third, when it comes to intimacy and not just talking about it, who at my age has the right to tell you at your age what to do? I can only say what I hope for you, not (necessarily) what I achieved for myself at your age. There is the matter of your own and your church's or synagogue's beliefs and values.

The religious traditions of this country and much of the world — Judaic, Islamic, Christian — regard sex as a means of sanctification, and deem sexual life within marriage to be holy. These beliefs, second, contradict not only the wild impulses of the late adolescent body but also the powerful pressures of late adolescent society, not only for sex, but for casual and serial relationships. A macho or a jock (or whatever term is in use) constantly talks about his prowess — and everyone else listens. Not surprisingly, young people in many instances find a conflict between the stated values of their upbringing and the conflicting doctrines of their age group (as well as a considerable part of public expression). How do you find your way through the pressures of society — both pro and con — and the pressures of your own heart, both yes and no? You know the answer better than I, for you lived with sexual conflicts long before you opened this book.

But the obvious needs saying, at least one more time. Do not exploit. Do not be exploited. Remember that sex is not out there but in here, in the deepest layer of your own being. There is not only a morning after — there are also lots of days and years afterward. I still believe that the most beautiful relationships between men and women last for a long time and entwine two hearts, two lives, as one. Sex is all day long because it takes so many forms, brings about so many moments of encounter. The sexual act is the climax of a whole relationship. That seems to me to state the ideal.

The other half of sex is gender. Here I have a great deal to say, and I stand on surer ground. I have been a feminist before feminism, because I grew up in a family of intelligent and assertive women and never realized women were supposed to be dumb and submissive. My grandmother ran a store and a real estate business, my mother published a newspaper, and — no surprise — the only women I could ever find attractive were brilliant, interesting, striking, lively. I married the most interesting woman I ever met. Only when I became a college teacher did I discover that other people did not see things this way. It took me some time to realize what I was seeing.

Too many girls speak quietly, do not contradict boys, seldom argue, and listen carefully. Too many girls write everything down and simply repeat it. Boys talk loudly, contradict and interrupt girls, prove contentious, and talk before they listen. Boys propose theories, explain things. When did I realize that that pattern governs the classroom? After about a decade of not noticing. The glory of the feminist movement for me and the reason I am a feminist flow from my calling as a teacher. I am too impatient to accept the intellectual timidity of the obviously brilliant woman, too cynical to accept the assertive ignorance of the stupid man.

I make equal demands on my students, men and women both, and set goals for them just a step beyond where they are. No surgeon can imagine treating a woman's broken leg differently from a man's, and no teacher should teach one student differently from the other either. But in the nature of things, that means that in order to do his or her job, every teacher must become a feminist. For men talk down to women, men ignore women, men interrupt women in the classroom, men favor women who say little (and do much). What this means in practical terms in the classroom is easy to say. Women have to talk up, speaking in voices that can be heard. They have to develop capacities for assertiveness in vigorous discourse and in their writing — using the subjunctive and the passive less (so to speak) and saying what they think in a straightforward way. Intellectually in the classroom there should be no difference between men and women. The society we hope to build requires the best of both halves of the population. It's that simple.

Do I claim that on today's campus women will find freedom to be themselves — to be women when they want, students when they want, intellectuals when they want, athletes when they want, whatever they want to be, wherever and whenever they want to be it? No, the opposite is the case. Women will have to develop their own criteria for judging classrooms and professors, colleges and universities, teaching the teachers how to serve all of their students. So far we have episodic lessons and a lot of guesswork.

When looking looking at colleges and universities, a woman student should note whether the curriculum includes courses in aspects of women's studies. She should also determine whether women occupy important positions in the administration and faculty. Third, she should learn whether women enjoy full equality with men in undergraduate activities, politics, sports, arts. These seem obvious and fundamental questions. Another generation will refine things.

There is also the matter of sexual harassment. Whenever someone pressures you to do something you do not want to do, that is harassment. When the pressure concerns sex, overt or covert, when a relationship shifts on account of sexual traits or desires present on either side, that constitutes sexual harassment. People generally assume women are harassed, men do the harassing. But that is not always so. When men are pressured to assume a sexual identity they do not find natural to themselves, one, for example, for which they are not yet ready, they too are harassed — and by well-meaning women at that. There is no sexual calendar to which we all must conform, any more than there is an intellectual one.

The problem of sexual harassment surely affects women more than men, and in more ways. Sexual harassment comes in the obvious forms of exchanges for sexual compliance. But I listed the more important forms when I discussed the ways in which teachers and students impose on women traits supposedly common to their sex, and prevent women from defining what they want to be on their own. That practice troubles me because it prevails, and women harass one another. On my campus the brilliant woman suffers from pressures not inflicted on the brilliant man. Gender traits may apply in general, but all of us have the right, still, to be free to be ourselves. Some day that sentence will seem insufferably banal. Today, alas, it is not.

Since we live in an age in which some people find their deepest relationships, including sexual ones, with their own sex, it remains to take note of the special problems faced by gays and lesbians and people who can enjoy sexual relations with both sexes. The bravest student I ever knew was the president of the Gay Students Alliance on my campus. This student publicly identified himself and stood up for what he believed to be right. But for other gay students, that kind of courage could produce unhappy results. These students are different, lonely, insecure, uncertain of the future. Few families accord to them the support and acceptance they most need. To be gay for many — too many — is to be the opposite of happy.

Our job as teachers is to serve all of our students in those areas of their lives in which we can be helpful to them. Our task in universities (to state matters negatively) is at least not to add to the burdens of people who do not think they fit into the norm — whether to be abnormal is to be black, a woman, a Buddhist, a follower of a newer religion ("cult"), a deeply believing Christian, a Jew, a conservative, or a liberal. And that goes, also, for gays and lesbians. No student faces a more difficult task than the student who has in unfamiliar ways to define his or her sexual identity and also sexual way of life.

Sex and gender — the center of our lives, the things that divide us and so unite us — also define the work of growing up. How we in higher education have managed all these years to pretend they do not exist I cannot say. For a long time some people imagined simply that people could best get an education in schools of all boys or all girls. Sex was not supposed to affect education at all. But it did. I left such a school because I found the ethos like that in a marine boot camp, with fine, sensitive young men pretending to be machos and jocks in order to survive. Yet even now we pretend that education can be complete without study of the place and meaning of gender in history and culture, analysis of the tension and conflict of gender in the entire cycle of life, from the earliest years to the grave. A full and complete sexual relationship completes man through woman, and woman through man: That is the ideal. But the reality isn't so bad either.

Chapter Nineteen

We Are What We Do

ET ME CLOSE WITH ANOTHER KIND OF commencement message, one to a group of freshmen commencing their studies at my university. Happily, this one made no headlines.

"This past summer, on July 28, 1982, to be exact, I turned fifty. When I was eighteen, twenty-five seemed old, and fifty, unattainable. When my children were younger and wanted to know about the past, they would ask me, 'And how were things when you were alive?' So, in all, the perspective of your generation upon the dotage of my generation is clear. No one here would willingly change ages with me. I don't blame you.

"But, for my part, I should not want to change ages with you. I should rather be fifty than any earlier age, but especially eighteen. If I tell you why, it is so that you may gain perspective on who you are, what work you have now to accomplish, and why, in general, you feel about yourselves the way you do: nervous and unsure.

"You are in the most difficult age of life, so far as I have lived it, and you confront, this very week as freshmen at our university, one of life's unsteady moments. A few days ago, you could not wait to see your parents leave if they brought you here, or to leave them if they took you to a plane or train. The adventure begins. Life begins. You begin. True enough, but once you left them and they you, a large emptiness filled your heart: loneliness in part, but uncertainty in still larger measure. Only when you learned to walk were you so prone to stumble as you are just now.

"And rightly so, for now you really are on your own. You should be on your own. It is the greatest gift your parents can give you. The good mother, the good father, loves the child, hugs and kisses him and her, explains how to cross the street — and then sends the child out to cross the street alone. If you and they are lucky, you will live to bury your parents, not they you. So even now you take the first steps toward life on your own, toward the age when you are orphans but also parents of your own children: responsible.

"You look outward into a clouded future. Think of the questions you have to answer and yet cannot: How shall I make a living? Whom shall I marry? What sort of life do I want to lead? At fifty I can answer all those questions; at eighteen, I could not even have imagined the right answers. All the definitions of yourselves lie before you. In the next four years you will have to look in books, relationships with others, and your own hearts and souls for answers.

"The gift lavished upon you by your parents and by this university and its teachers, and by others who help pay for your education, is the chance to fail without becoming a failure, to make mistakes without turning into a loser, to guess wrong without result. Here we give you the chance to experiment with life, yet not get cut if the test tube blows up in your face. Here, then, is your last chance in life to try things out without ongoing, awful consequences.

"When I was a freshman in college, I went out for the fencing team, for two ghastly days, and for the soccer team for one more. Then I discovered God wanted me to be a writer, not a fencer. So I took a creative writing course. My classmate, John Updike, got an A, and I got a B. So I decided God wanted Updike to be a writer. I was meant for something else. I can't remember just now what I thought it was. It does not seem important anymore.

"So you too have the chance to take any number of subjects you did not know existed. You can try out for sports you have never played. You can meet kinds of people you have never met before, for instance, blacks if you are white, whites if you are black. You can enter into relationships of a sort you have not known, nurture friends of diverse sorts, learn to love and respect people quite differently from the ways you now know.

"And when you make a mistake, for one last time, you do not have to defend it, repeat it, or suffer forever on account of it. You need only learn from it. That is the power and the pleasure of your college years, the bridge from home to the great world beyond that only the most fortunate young people get to cross.

"Since, as I told you, I am two months into the second half century of life, indulge an old man and listen to some good advice. My oldest son goes to college next year. He won't listen to my good advice, so you will have to.

"The people who really love you here, who care about what you learn and how you grow, and who take pride in their work and measure their success by your achievement — those people will not give you easy courses. They will not give you easy grades. They will not hand out much praise or encouragement, except when you earn the praise and, by your serious effort, show you deserve encouragement.

"Many teachers (though not all) live for what they do, and what they do is teach you. Have patience with us zealots of the mind, us extremists in the nurture of the intellect. Moderation in the life of the mind is no virtue. Extremism in pursuit of the mature intellect is no vice.

"It is easy to seek the easier type of course, where you may relax, write things down, say them back on exams or papers, and pull off a decent grade. But we learn only by discovering and doing. We learn best by doing the hardest things. You will learn and grow only by doing for yourself things you have never known lay within your grasp. You will become more than what you are only by reaching upward beyond the place you thought you could touch: We are what we do.

"We have worked to create a way of learning at this university that makes possible the kinds of risks I recommend. The curriculum leaves you more free choice than you would find in any other university in the country. You therefore bear responsibility for yourselves. What criteria will guide you in making choices? How, at eighteen or nineteen, can you decide questions that trouble people two or three times your age? These burdens of life today come to rest upon your shoulders. Choosing courses, friends, things to do, ways to spend your time and enjoy life — these choices now face you, and for the first time in your lives, you alone can answer them. Now create yourself afresh: We are what we do.

"Now comes the first exercise at living on your own, as I said: a chance to learn by doing, yet not to come to destruction if you fail. When you succeed, as you will, you will be ready for that next range of questions: How shall I make a living? Whom shall I marry? What sort of life do I want to lead? Once you have succeeded in answering the questions of this week, this month, this year, you will rightly trust yourself and rely on yourself to take up the questions of tomorrow. We are what we do.

"I've given you plenty of advice, and I close with Neusner's Law. It is this: When in doubt, lie. I mean, *do not let people put you down.*

"Believe in yourself and stand for yourself and trust yourself. Your own judgment, for you, must govern — even in the face of stern advice from fifty-year-old professors."

Index

of the Growing Person, 19

Students
anticipating professionalism,
27-31
capacity for college study,
69-74
development of disciplined
learning, 5-13
expectations, 62
experimentation to establish
identity, 15-21
friendship and sex, 147-152
junior year outlooks, 137-142
"major" as "field of
concentration," 95-103
maturity through learning,
15-21
preparation for post-college
life, 89-94
"shopping" for education,
75-88
transition from high school
to college, 131-136

Teaching assistants, role of,
108-111
Tenure, effect of, 111-113

University
administration and teaching,
115-122
junior year election as
challenge, 137-142
"major" as "field of
concentration," 95-103
role in preparation and
performance, 5-13
social importance of, 1-2
social values and learning of,
123-128
Upper classmen
"major," election of and
junior year outlooks,
overseas study, 137-142
outward look of seniors,
143-145

Washington Post, The, 48
Wilson, Woodrow, 117
Wriston, Henry, 118

Jacob Neusner (pronounced News-ner) has taught at Brown University, the most popular school in the Ivy League, for sixteen years. In 1981, Professor Neusner made headlines when he criticized students and his fellow teachers for lowering their standards and wasting the precious four years of college. In this book, Neusner reflects on those criticisms and offers advise to students who are striving for the best that college has to offer.